How Now Shall We Live?
Collegiate Edition

ISBN 0-6330-0456-1

Dewey Decimal Classification: 248.834
Subject Heading: CHRISTIAN LIFE \ COLLEGE STUDENTS \ SALVATION

Unless otherwise noted, Scripture quotations are from the Holy Bible,
New International Version, copyright © 1973, 1978, 1984
by International Bible Society.

Order additional copies of this book by writing to Customer Service Center, MSN 113;
127 Ninth Avenue, North; Nashville, TN 37234-0113; by calling toll free (800) 458-2772;
by faxing (615) 251-5933; by ordering online at www.lifeway.com; by emailing
customerservice@lifeway.com; or by visiting a LifeWay Christian Store.

National Collegiate Ministry Department
LifeWay Christian Resources
127 Ninth Avenue North
Nashville, TN 37234-0153
Customer Service: (800) 458-2772

Printed in the United States of America

Editor : Art Herron
Art Direction and Design : Edward Crawford
Cover and Theme Illustration : Richard Tuschman
Assistant Editor : Leanne Lawrence

LifeWay.

LifeWay Press
127 Ninth Avenue, North
Nashville, Tennessee 37234-0152

As God works through us, we will help people and churches know Jesus Christ and seek His
kingdom by providing biblical solutions that spiritually transform individuals and cultures.

How Now Shall We Live?
Collegiate Edition

Charles Colson
and Nancy Pearcey & Bill Henry

LifeWay Press
Nashville, Tennessee

Contents

Introduction

Centuries ago, when the Jews were in exile, in the depths of despair, they cried out to God, "How should we then live?" The same question still rings down through the ages. How shall we live—today?

The new millennium marks an extraordinary opportunity for the church. After two thousand years, the birth of the Son of God still remains the defining moment of history. Jesus founded a church that could not be destroyed—not by his own crucifixion or by his followers' deaths in the Colosseum, not by the barbarian hoards, or by mighty Turkish emperors, not by modern tyrants or by the power of sophisticated ideologies you learn about on the campus.

After two thousand years, we can affirm that Jesus Christ is indeed the same yesterday, today and forever. This alone should make the opening decade of the millennium cause for jubilation, a time when Christians on the college campus boldly and confidently recommit themselves to engage contemporary culture with a fresh vision of hope. Yet my sense is that most Christians on the campus are anything but jubilant, and for good reason.

We live in a culture that is at best morally indifferent. A culture in which Christian values are mocked and when immorality in high places is not only ignored but even rewarded in the voting booth. A culture in which violence, banality, meanness, and disintegrating personal behavior are destroying civility and endangering the very life of the campus community. A culture in which the most profound moral dilemmas are addressed by the cold logic of utilitarianism.

What's more, when Christians do make good-faith efforts to halt this slide into barbarism, we are maligned as intolerant or bigoted. Small wonder that many students have concluded that the "culture war" is over—and that we lost the battle on campus. Battle weary, we are tempted to withdraw into the safety of our church, fellowship group or even a sports group hoping to find relief.

Turning our back as college students on the impact we can and must have on our culture is a betrayal of our biblical mandate and our own heritage as Christians. Why? Because it denies God's sovereignty over all of life. Nothing could be more ill-timed or more deadly for our Christian walk with Christ. To abandon the battlefield now is to desert the cause just when we are seeing the first signs that historic Christianity may be on the verge of a great breakthrough. The process of secularization begun in the Enlightenment is grinding to a halt. All the ideologies, all the utopian promises that have marked this century have proven utterly bankrupt.

University students have achieved what modernism presented as life's great shining purpose: individual autonomy, the right to do what one chooses. Yet this has not produced the promised freedom, the peace of mind we seek. We have discovered that we cannot live with the chaos that inevitably results from choice divorced from morality. As a result, college students are groping for something that will restore the shattered bonds of community, something that will make sense of life. If the Christian faith turns inward now, if we focus only on our own needs, we will miss the opportunity to provide answers at a time when people are sensing a deep longing for meaning and order.

As we will argue in these pages, Christianity offers the only viable, rationally defensible answers to these questions. Only Christianity offers a way to understand the physical and moral order. Only Christianity offers a comprehensive worldview that covers all areas of life and thought, every aspect of creation. Only Christianity offers a way to live in response to these realities.

God exists. He has spoken. He is revealed in Christ, the Alpha and the Omega. He is sovereign over all creation. Consequently, as a Christian student, you must see Christianity as a life system, or worldview, that governs every area of existence and speaks to both the moral and the physical order of the universe. In many respects, we have failed in the church to help you understand this as you enter college.

This failure has been crippling in many ways. For one thing, we cannot answer the questions our friends discover by attending classes every day. We are incapable of preparing our friends to answer the challenges they face. For ourselves, we cannot explain to our friends and classmates why we believe, and we often cannot defend our faith when we are challenged.

Most of all, our failure to see Christianity as a comprehensive framework of truth has crippled our efforts to have a redemptive effect on the surrounding culture on campus and off campus. At its most fundamental level, the so-called "culture war" is a clash of belief systems. It is, as Kuyper put it, a clash of principle against principle, of worldview against worldview. Only when we see this can we effectively evangelize a post-Christian culture, bringing God's righteousness to bear in the world around us.

That is why Nancy Pearcey, Bill Henry, Jerry Pounds and I felt compelled to write this workbook: to present Christianity as a total worldview and life system, to help believers on the campus discover its truth and live accordingly, and to equip you to communicate the great truths of the faith and seize the magnificent opportunity of the new millennium—to be nothing less than God's agents in building a new Christian culture.

I am grateful to Dr. Bill Henry and Dr. Jerry Pounds for the sensitivity they have brought to our developing this workbook. Dr. Henry is the director of National Collegiate Ministry at LifeWay Christian Resources of the Southern Baptist Convention. He has devoted his entire professional career to ministering to the college community. Dr. Jerry Pounds is a collegiate writer and speaker. As a professor at New Orleans Baptist Theological Seminary, he is constantly influencing the leaders of the church on a daily basis. Both men have taken my work and shaped it to be relevant and easy to use on the college campus. Both are committed to helping develop a Christian worldview for you as a college student.

Get Ready!

Welcome to an exciting study in understanding the meaning and origin of your faith in Jesus Christ. If you have picked up this book for study and are not a Christian, it is my desire that you earnestly seek to know Him as your Lord and Savior. The basic premise of this book is that Jesus Christ is the God who brought all of creation into existence, yourself included. Doesn't it stand to reason that if a God who loves you gives you life in the physical sense, He desires to give you eternal life? If you are a professed Christian and not sure about your salvation, seek out a believer in Christ and confirm your salvation as the two of you open the Bible and seek God's truth.

This study is an interactive approach to God's timely truth. Throughout the book you will find numerous examples of how you can interact with the text. As you encounter these items within the text, see them as opportunities to open a new avenue to understanding God. They will slow your reading down when they are encountered. This is intentional, for each interactive tool can be viewed as a moment to pause and think. Therefore, when you encounter text in a sidebar or questions, use them. Do what is called for. Once you have paused and reflected, then continue on with the text.

The items you are likely to encounter are sidebar quotes, questions seeking an answer which you are to write out, pictures and icons which speak a message, many times without words. Each of the six sessions are broken into five individual Bible studies. At the end of each Bible study you will find additional opportunities for dialogue with the writers through "Points to Remember," "Questions to Ask," "Actions to Take," and "Prayers to Pray."

As you study, it will be helpful for you to have a copy of the Holy Bible. You will need one which contains both the Old and New Testaments. When you are instructed to read a passage of Scripture, it is always in bold format. The text will be from either the Old or New Testaments. If you are not familiar with the Bible, go to the index page to find a particular book of the Bible.

If you are using this study in a small group setting, take time to get to know the other members of your group. As you share your thoughts and feelings with them throughout the study, it will be helpful to be able to share with one another as friends.

Teaching Helps

If you are a group leader and need additional teaching helps, these are available to you free upon request at National Collegiate Ministry, 127 Ninth Avenue, North, Nashville, TN 37234. You may also call 615-251-2777 (CST). Although not needed for individual study, the teaching helps address how the collegiate material may be taught in a group setting, and they also deal with group dynamics.

Get ready for an exciting journey of faith. Our thanks to Chuck Colson and the others who contributed to this spiritual tool directed to you as a collegian or young adult.

The Editor

Indistinguishable Christians?

How can your friends tell if you are a Christian if your actions communicate a secular lifestyle? In this session you will examine both the secular worldview and the Biblical worldview.

DAY ONE
Discover Your Worldview

"Guide me in your truth and teach me, for you are God my Savior, and my hope is in you all day long" (Psalm 25:5).

Centuries ago, when the Jews were in exile, in the depths of despair, they cried out to God, "How should we then live?" The same question still rings down through the ages. How shall we live today?

"Christians are virtually indistinguishable from non-believers in terms of lifestyle. How can this be with so much teaching going on? It has finally struck me that without a biblical worldview, all the great teaching goes in one ear and out the other. There are no intellectual pegs… no biblical pegs… in the mind of the individual to hang these truths on. So they just pass through. They don't stick. They don't make a difference." —George Barna

In a brief sentence, write out how you think the world would answer the question "How shall we live today?" _____
_____
_____
_____

Now, in a brief sentence write out how you think the following groups would answer this same question.

Parents _____
_____
_____
_____
_____

School Administrators _____
_____
_____
_____

Faculty_____
_____
_____
_____

Greek Fraternities/Sororities _____
_____
_____
_____

Freshmen _____
_____
_____
_____

Graduating Seniors _____
_____
_____
_____

From what you know of God's Word and from your relationship with God, how would God answer this question? _____
_____
_____
_____
_____

Today, we have entered the millennium that marks the 2000th anniversary of the birth of Jesus—an extraordinary moment for the Christian church. After two thousand years, the birth of the Son of God still remains the defining moment of history.

Jesus founded a church that could not be destroyed—not by His own crucifixion or by His followers' deaths in the Colosseum, not by barbarian hoards or mighty Turkish emperors, not by modern tyrants or the power of sophisticated ideologies. After two thousand years, we can affirm that Jesus Christ is indeed the same yesterday, today, and forever. This alone should make the opening decade of the millennium cause for jubilation, a time when college Christians boldly and confidently recommit themselves to engaging contemporary culture with a fresh vision of hope.

In what ways have you seen Christians on the campus engage our culture with hope? _____
_____
_____
_____
_____
_____

Yet my sense is that most Christians on the campus are anything but jubilant. And for good reason. We experience some of the same sense of exile that the Jews did in the time of Ezekiel. We live in a culture that is at best morally indifferent. A culture in which Judeo-Christian values are mocked and where immorality in high places is not only ignored but even rewarded in the voting booth. A culture in which violence, banality, meanness, and disintegrating personal behavior are destroying civility and endangering the very life of our communities. A culture in which the most profound moral dilemmas are addressed by the cold logic of utilitarianism.

Take a moment to look at TV or in your newspaper and identify ways our culture is becoming more violent and immoral. List some of these here. _____
_____
_____
_____
_____

(The next time you read your campus newspaper, see if any of these issues are addressed.)

As a result, Americans are groping for something that will restore the shattered bonds of campus community, something that will make sense of life. If the church turns inward now, if we focus only on our own needs, we will miss the opportunity to provide answers at a time when students are sensing a deep longing for meaning and order. It is not enough to focus exclusively on the spiritual, on Bible studies and evangelistic campaigns, while turning a blind eye to the distinctive tensions of contemporary life. We must show the world that Christianity is more than a private belief, more than personal salvation. We must show that it is a comprehensive life system that answers all of humanity's age-old questions.

Answer some of these questions below:

Where did I come from? _____
_____
_____

Why am I here? _____
_____
_____

Where am I going? _____
_____
_____

Does life have any meaning and purpose?
_____
_____
_____

As we will argue in these pages, Christianity offers the only viable, rationally defensible answers to these questions. Only Christianity offers a way to understand the physical and moral order. Only Christianity offers a comprehensive

We live in a culture that is at best morally indifferent.

At its most fundamental level, the so-called "culture war" is a clash of belief systems. It is, as Kuyper put it, a clash of principle against principle, of worldview against worldview.

worldview that covers all areas of life and thought, every aspect of creation. Only Christianity offers a way to live in response to these realities. God exists. He has spoken. He is revealed in Christ, the Alpha and Omega. He is sovereign over all creation.

STATEMENT The church's singular failure in recent decades has been the failure to see Christianity as a life system, or worldview, that governs every area of existence and speaks to both the moral and the physical order of the universe. And this failure has been crippling in many ways. For one thing, our parents struggled in answering the questions we, as children, brought home from school, so they were incapable of preparing us to answer the challenges we face. For ourselves, we cannot explain to our friends and classmates why we believe, and we often cannot defend our faith when we are challenged. We do not know how to organize our lives correctly. We live in the dark, allowing our lives to be shaped by the world around us. What's more, by failing to see Christian truth in every aspect of life, we miss so much beauty and meaning in our own lives: the thrill of seeing God's splendor in the intricacies of nature, or hearing His voice in the performance of a great symphony, or detecting His character in the harmony of a well-ordered community.

Think about your own life. Is the above paragraph true for you?
❏ Yes   ❏ No

If yes, then how is it so? _____
_____
_____
_____
_____
_____
_____

If no, how is it different? _____
_____
_____
_____

Most of all, our failure to see Christianity as a comprehensive framework of truth has crippled our efforts to have a redemptive effect on the surrounding culture. At its most fundamental level, the so-called "culture war" is a clash of belief systems. It is, as Kuyper put it, a clash of principle against principle, of worldview against worldview. Only when we see this can we effectively evangelize a post-Christian culture, bringing God's righteousness to bear in the world around us.

We are all familiar with saving grace; it is the means by which God's power calls people who are dead in their trespasses and sins to new life in Christ. But we rarely really understand common grace, which is the means by which God's power sustains creation, holding back the sin and evil that result from the Fall and that would otherwise overwhelm His creation like a great flood.

In your own words, what do you understand common grace to mean? _____
_____
_____
_____

As God's servants, acting in obedience to Him, we may at times be agents of either saving grace or common grace. As God's servant, His agent, what does that mean to you?

As an agent of God's saving grace, I _____
_____
_____
_____

As an agent of God's common grace, I _____
_____
_____
_____

As agents of God's common grace, we are called to help sustain and renew His creation, to uphold the created institutions of family and society, to pursue science and scholarship, to create works of art and beauty, to heal and help those suffering from the results of the Fall.

That is why we felt compelled to write this book:

a. to present Christianity as a total worldview and life system;

b. to help believers discover its truth and live accordingly;

c. to equip them to communicate the great truths of the faith and seize the magnificent opportunity of the new millennium—to be nothing less than God's agents in building a new Christian culture.

List the three main purposes for this book:

1. _____
_____

2. _____
_____

3. _____
_____

Turn to Psalm 25 and answer the following questions.

How did David feel toward God? (v. 2)

_____

What were two things David asked of God? (v. 2) _____ and _____
_____

What four things did David want God to do? (vv. 4-5)

_____,
_____,
_____, and
_____

What relationship did David have with God? (v. 5)_____
_____

Because God was David's salvation, what was David willing to do all day? (v. 5)_____
_____
_____

Read Psalms 26:3; 30:9; 40:10,11; 43:3; 71:22; and 86:11.

What emphasis was David placing on his relationship with God? _____
_____
_____

✅ Points to Remember
List two key points of today's session.

1. _____
_____

2. _____
_____

❓ Questions to Ask
What questions do I have concerning what I've read today? _____
_____
_____
_____

👥 Actions to Take
Based on what I've read, what specific action(s) should I take? _____
_____
_____
_____

✴ Prayers to Pray
Today, God, you taught me _____
_____
_____
_____
_____
_____

Help me, Lord, to _____
_____
_____
_____

DAY TWO
Three Basic Questions

"Yet to all who received him, to those who believed in his name, he gave the right to become children of God" (John 1:12).

Genuine Christianity is a way of seeing and comprehending all reality. It is a worldview.

Our choices are shaped by what we believe is real and true, right and wrong, good and beautiful. Our choices are shaped by our worldview. A person's worldview is intensely practical. It is simply the sum total of our beliefs about the world, the "big picture" that directs our daily decisions and actions.

Every worldview can be analyzed by the way it answers three basic questions: Where did we come from and who are we (*creation*)? What has gone wrong with the world (*fall*)? And what can we do to fix it (*redemption*)? These three questions form a grid that we can use to break down the inner logic of every belief system or philosophy that we encounter.

Draw a line from each question to its appropriate key word:

Who are we?   **Redemption**

What has gone wrong with the world?   **Creation**

What can we do to fix it?

Where did we come from?   **Fall**

For the past few centuries, the secular world has asserted a dichotomy between science and religion, between fact and value, between objective knowledge and subjective feeling. As a result, Christians often think in terms of the same false dichotomy, allowing our belief system to be reduced to little more than private feelings and experience, completely divorced from objective facts. But this emphasis on a personal relationship can also be evangelicalism's greatest weakness, because it may prevent us from seeing God's plan for us beyond our personal salvation. Genuine Christianity is a way of seeing and comprehending all reality. It is a worldview.

In your own words, what has the secular world asserted? _____
_____
_____
_____
_____

Has this affected the way you witness? Why or why not?_____
_____
_____
_____
_____

The scriptural basis for saying this is the creation account, where we are told that God spoke everything into being out of nothing (see Genesis 1).

Mark the following statements true or false (T or F):
_____**Everything that exists came into being at God's command.**
_____**Not everything God created is subject to Him.**
_____**Everything God created finds its purpose and meaning in Him.**

_____Truth is found only in relationship to God and His revelation.

_____God created the natural world and natural laws.

_____God created our bodies and the moral laws.

_____God created our minds and the laws of logic and imagination.

_____God created us as social beings and gave us the principles for social and political institutions.

_____God created a world of beauty and the principles of aesthetics and artistic creation.

_____God's laws and ordinances have little to do with shaping how we should live.

Check your answers by reading the following paragraph.

STATEMENT Everything that exists came into being at His command and is therefore subject to Him, finding its purpose and meaning in Him. The implication is that in every topic we investigate, from ethics to economics to ecology, the truth is found only in relationship to God and His revelation. It is God who created the natural world and natural laws. God created our bodies and the moral laws that keep us healthy. God created our minds and the laws of logic and imagination. God created us as social beings and gave us the principles for social and political institutions. God created a world of beauty and the principles of aesthetics and artistic creation. In every area of life, genuine knowledge means not only discerning the laws and ordinances by which God has structured creation, but also allowing those laws to shape how we should live.

As the church fathers used to say, all truth is God's truth. That comprehensive truth is embodied in Christ, who is our Savior and yet also much more.

In the first chapter of John, Christ is called the "logos" (John 1:1). What does this word mean? _____

In the Greek, *logos* literally means the idea, the word, the rational pattern of creation, the order of the universe. The apostle Paul expands on this: "For by him all things were created: things in heaven and on earth, visible and invisible . . . ; all things were created by him and for him. He is before all things, and in him all things hold together" (Col.1:16-17). Jesus Himself is the word that God spoke to create the world (see Gen. 1).

Perhaps the most astonishing claim Jesus makes is, "I am the way and the truth and the life" (John 14:6). Jesus is the origin and end of all things, the Alpha and Omega. Nothing has meaning apart from Him. Nothing exists apart from Him. He is the Agent of creation, Author of all that is and ever will be. Christ is Lord over all of creation, from the human soul to the vast reaches of the cosmos.

Read Psalm 2; Psalm 8; Psalm 110; and Philippians 2:5-11.

What do these verses say about Christ and creation?_____
_____
_____
_____
_____
_____
_____

We are compelled to see that the Christian faith cannot be reduced to John 3:16 or simple formulas. Christianity cannot be limited merely to one component of our lives, a mere religious practice or observance, or even a salvation experience. We are compelled to see Christianity as the all-encompassing truth, the root of everything else. It is ultimate reality.

We are compelled to see Christianity as the all-encompassing truth, the root of everything else. It is ultimate reality.

The only way to live a rational and healthy life is to ascertain the nature of these divine laws and ordinances and then to use them as the basis for how we should live.

Our calling is not only to order our own lives by divine principles but also to engage the world.

If you have not made a decision to follow Christ and to make Him Lord over all, would you be willing to do so now? God knows you. You can know Him. Follow this simple outline:

a) Admit that you are a sinner (Read Romans 3:10-12, 23).

b) Realize the penalty for your sin (Read Romans 6:23).

c) Acknowledge payment God made for your sin (Read Romans 5:8).

d) Confess Jesus as your Lord and ask God to save you (Read Romans 10:9, 10, 13).

After reading these verses, are you willing to make the decision to trust Him now? If so, pray this prayer out loud. God hears your words wherever you are.

Dear God:
I know You love me. I realize that I am a sinner and that I have not lived the way You would want me to live. I believe that Jesus died on the cross for me, and He was raised from death to provide forgiveness and eternal life. I ask that You save me as I turn from my sins. I place my faith in You and receive You as my Lord and Savior. Give me the strength to live for You. Thank You for saving me and giving me eternal life. I pray this in Jesus' name. Amen.

If you prayed this prayer, share your decision with your leader or a Christian friend.

As a believer in Christ, understanding Christianity as a total life system is absolutely essential for both us and the church for two reasons. First, it enables us to make sense of the world we live in and thus order our lives more rationally. Second, it enables us to understand forces hostile to our faith, equipping us to evangelize and to defend Christian truth as God's instrument for transforming culture.

List these two reasons in your own words:
1. _____

_____

2. _____

_____

Because the world was created by an intelligent **Being**, rather than by chance, it has an intelligible order. The only way to live a rational and healthy life is to ascertain the nature of these divine laws and ordinances and then use them as the basis for how we should live.

This understanding of life's laws is what Scripture calls wisdom. How would you define wisdom? _____

_____

_____

_____

"Wisdom in Scripture is, broadly speaking, the knowledge of God's world and the knack of fitting oneself into it," writes Calvin College professor Cornelius Plantinga. A wise person is one who knows the boundaries and limits, the laws and rhythms and seasons of the created order, both in the physical and the social world. "To be wise is to know reality and then accommodate yourself to it." To deny God is to blind ourselves to reality, and the inevitable consequence is that we will bump up against reality in painful ways, just as a blindfolded driver will crash into other drivers or run off the road.

Our calling is not only to order our own lives by divine principles but also to engage the world. We are commanded both to preach the good news and to bring all things into submission to God's order, by defending and living out God's truth in the unique historical and cultural conditions of our age.

In what ways are you engaging the world? __

_____

_____

_____

_____

_____

How would you evaluate what you are doing? _____ (Write in a number using the scale below.)

1 2 3 4 5 6 7 8 9 10

DON'T EVEN ASK!   SOME EFFORT   SEEING POSITIVE RESULTS!

To engage the world requires that we understand the great ideas that compete for people's minds and hearts. The most fundamental weakness in modern evangelicalism is that we've been fighting cultural skirmishes on all sides without knowing what the war itself is about. The culture war is not just about abortion, homosexual rights, or the decline of public education. These are only the skirmishes. The real war is a cosmic struggle between worldviews—between the Christian worldview and the various secular and spiritual worldviews arrayed against it.

(Fill in these blanks.)
If we are going to be effective in both evangelizing our world today and transforming it to reflect the wisdom of the Creator, then we must understand that the real war is between _____ views and the _____ _____ view.

Turn to John 1:1-14 and answer the following questions:

Who was the Word? (v. 1)_____
_____

Who was with God in the beginning? (v. 1)___
_____

What did Jesus do? (v. 3) _____
_____

What do verses 4-11 say about Jesus? _____
_____
_____
_____
_____
_____

How does one receive Christ (v. 12)? (Refer back to the earlier points and the prayer about becoming a Christian)._____
_____
_____
_____
_____
_____
_____
_____
_____
_____
_____

✅ Points to Remember
List two key points of today's session.
1._____
_____
2._____
_____

❓ Questions to Ask
What questions do I have concerning what I've read today? _____
_____
_____
_____

🐾 Actions to Take
Based on what I've read, what specific action(s) should I take? _____
_____
_____

✳ Prayers to Pray
Today, God, you taught me _____
_____
_____
_____
_____

Help me, Lord, to _____
_____
_____
_____
_____

The culture war is not just about abortion, homosexual rights, or the decline of public education. These are only the skirmishes. The real war is a cosmic struggle between worldviews— between the Christian worldview and the various secular and spiritual worldviews arrayed against it.

DAY THREE
Theism vs Naturalism

"Since ancient times no one has heard, no ear has perceived, no eye has seen any God besides you, who acts on behalf of those who wait for him" (Isaiah 64:4).

What is the major challenge today? In the broadest categories, the conflict of our day is theism versus naturalism. **Theism** believes in a transcendent God who created the universe; **naturalism** believes that natural causes alone are sufficient to explain everything that exists. The conflict voices itself in foundational questions.

Your roommate has asked you the following questions. How would you answer each one?

Is ultimate reality God or the cosmos? _____
_____
_____
_____

Is there a supernatural realm, or is nature all that exists? _____
_____
_____
_____

Has God spoken and revealed His truth to us, or is truth something we have to find, even invent, for ourselves?_____
_____
_____
_____

Is there a purpose to our lives, or are we cosmic accidents emerging from the slime? ____
_____
_____
_____

When it comes to moral issues, naturalism results in relativism. If nature is all there is, then there is no transcendent source of truth or morality. Truth is relative, and we are left to construct morality on our own. Every principle is reduced to a personal preference. By contrast, the Christian believes in a God who has spoken, who has revealed an absolute and unchanging standard of right and wrong, based ultimately on His own holy character.

Since naturalists deny any transcendent moral standards, they tend toward a pragmatic approach. Pragmatism says: Whatever works best is right. Why does this contradict what Christians believe? _____
_____
_____
_____
_____
_____
_____
_____

Actions and policies are judged on utilitarian grounds alone. By contrast, the Christian could be called an idealist, judging actions not by what works but by what ought to be, based on God's standards. Naturalists generally embrace the Enlightenment notion that human nature is essentially good, which leads to utopianism. Utopianism says: If only we create the right social and economic structures, we can usher in an age of harmony and prosperity.

Give one reason why this contradicts what Christians believe. _____

_____

_____

_____

If we are going to make a difference in our world, we must grasp these profoundly contrary views of reality, for what people believe on this fundamental level is at the root of our cultural crisis. The dominant worldview today is naturalism, which has created a culture that is both post-Christian and postmodernist. By *post-Christian* we mean that Americans, and indeed most Western cultures, no longer rely on Judeo-Christian truths as the basis of their public philosophy or their moral consensus.

How have you seen this...
In our nation? _____

_____

_____

_____

In our government? _____

_____

_____

_____

On your campus? _____

_____

_____

_____

Can you identify two other examples of our world becoming more post-Christian?

Example 1: _____

_____

_____

_____

Example 2: _____

_____

_____

_____

Today's culture not only is post-Christian but also is rapidly becoming postmodernist, which means it is resistant not only to Christian truth claims but to any truth claims. *Postmodernism* rejects any objective reality and poses an ominous threat both to democratic discourse and to our ability to sustain a moral order in society.

In the 1960s the percentage of young people going to college suddenly surged, and attitudes once held only by the intellectual elite suddenly became common coinage. The philosophy of *existentialism*, a precursor of postmodernism, swept the campuses, proclaiming that life is absurd, meaningless, and that the individual self must create his own meaning. Choice was elevated to the ultimate value, the only justification for any actions.

What evidence existing on your campus can you trace back to a philosophy of existentialism? _____

_____

_____

Postmodernism argues that all viewpoints, all lifestyles, all beliefs and behaviors are regarded as equally valid. Institutions of higher learning have embraced this philosophy so aggressively that they have adopted campus codes enforcing political correctness. Tolerance has become so important that no exception is tolerated.

Are there groups on your campus addressing all viewpoints? ❏ Yes ❏ No

If so, what lifestyles are recognized by these groups? _____

_____

_____

_____

In the past, Christian students proclaiming their faith might expect to encounter a vigorous debate over the rational grounds

Institutions of higher learning have embraced this philosophy so aggressively that they have adopted campus codes enforcing political correctness. Tolerance has become so important that no exception is tolerated.

for belief; but today the same message is likely to be met with bored indifference. This is exactly the attitude I witnessed when I spoke at Yale Law School in 1996. Before my lecture, I dined with Professor Stephen Carter, the brilliant Yale legal scholar and committed Christian. Over a plate of enchiladas in a small campus hangout, I told him of my apprehensions.

"Don't worry about a riot," he chuckled. "They'll listen quietly and walk away without saying a word." "But I'm going to tell them that there can be no basis for law without a Christian consensus, or at least a recognition of natural law," I said.

Carter smiled patiently. "When these students come to Yale, they are taught that the law has nothing to do with morality. And they accept that. So you can have your opinions, and they'll find those interesting, but they won't even bother to argue."

As I spoke, I searched the students' eyes, hoping for some sign of engagement. Nothing. As I progressed into my material, I became more provocative, but they remained impassive.

During the question-and-answer period, no one challenged a single premise I had advanced. Most of the queries came from the Christians in the front rows. Carter had sized up his students well. They listened politely, took a few notes, then packed up their papers and quietly slipped out of the auditorium.

Debate can be unpleasant at times, but at least it presupposes that there are truths worth defending, ideas worth fighting for. But in our postmodernist age, your truths are yours, my truths are mine, and none are significant enough to get passionate about. And if there is no truth, then we cannot persuade one another by rational arguments.

How do you think your school would have responded to such a talk? _____
_____
_____

Across the country, a generation of college graduates have marched off, degrees in their hands and a postmodernist ideology in their heads, to work in the nation's executive suites, in political centers, and the editorial rooms of newspapers, magazines, and television studios. The result has been the emergence of a new and influential group of professionals who work primarily with words and ideas—what some sociologists call the New Class or the knowledge class or, more derogatorily, the chattering class. And because they control the means of public discourse, their philosophy has become dominant. The worldview framed on campuses from the 1960s on is now in the mainstream of American life.

How does this viewpoint relate to your own campus?

1	2	3	4	5	6	7	8	9	10

IT'S NOT ACCURATE   SOME TRUTH TO IT   RIGHT ON TARGET!

Christians on the campus must understand the clash of worldviews that is changing the face of American society so we will stand ready to respond as people grow disillusioned with false beliefs and values and as they begin to seek for real answers. We must know not only what our worldview is and why we believe it but also how to explain that worldview and defend it. We must also have some understanding of the opposing worldviews and why people believe them. Only then can we present the gospel in language in which it can be understood. Only then can we defend truth in a way that is winsome and persuasive.

Reread the above paragraph. In one concise sentence, rewrite these thoughts in your own words. _____
_____
_____
_____
_____

Check how will you respond to this challenge.
___Someone else will do it!
___I'll help if someone else leads.
___I'm indifferent.
___I'll think about it.
___I'm ready to respond for Christ!
___(other response) _____

Turn to Isaiah 64:1-8 and answer the following questions:

What will God do for those who remember His ways? (v. 5) _____
_____
_____
_____

What is our righteousness compared to? (v. 6)
_____
_____
_____
_____

What have our iniquities done for us? (vv. 6-7)
_____
_____
_____
_____

What is our relationship to God? (v. 8) _____
_____
_____
_____

What analogy is offered? (v. 8) _____
_____
_____
_____
_____

Who are we? (v. 8) _____
_____
_____
_____
_____

✅ Points to Remember
List two key points of today's session.
1. _____
_____
2. _____
_____

❓ Questions to Ask
What questions do I have concerning what I've read today? _____
_____
_____
_____

👥 Actions to Take
Based on what I've read, what specific action(s) should I take? _____
_____
_____

✳️ Prayers to Pray
Today, God, you taught me _____
_____
_____
_____
_____

Help me, Lord, to _____
_____
_____
_____

DAY FOUR
Intellectual Evangelism

"Therefore, I urge you, brothers, in view of God's mercy, to offer your bodies as living sacrifices, holy and pleasing to God—this is your spiritual act of worship" (Romans 12:1).

The Jews were steeped in the Old Testament Scriptures. They knew there was one God, and that He was the Creator; they understood sin and guilt and sacrifice; they looked forward to the coming Messiah. As a result, the apostles were able to approach them by beginning with the message that Christ was, in fact, the awaited Messiah.

> False ideas are the greatest obstacles to the reception of the gospel. We may preach with all the fervor of a reformer and yet succeed only in winning a straggler here or there, if we permit the whole collective thought of a nation or of the world to be controlled by ideas which by the resistless force of logic, prevent Christianity from being regarded as anything more than a harmless delusion. —J. Gresham Machen

But the Greeks had no knowledge of Scripture, and the concepts of sin and guilt and redemption were not familiar to them. Their concept of "god" was a pantheon of deities who operated from human passions, merely on a grander scale. As a result, the apostles had to find a different starting point. The classic example is Paul's speech on Mars Hill in Athens (located in the Bible, Acts 17). As a springboard, Paul referred to one of the city's religious sites, an altar that bore the inscription "To an unknown god." Later he quoted Greek poetry: "As some of your own poets have said, 'We

are his offspring'" (Acts 17:28).

What was the purpose of Paul appealing to the Greeks' own experiences and literature?

_____

_____

_____

Paul appealed to his audience's own experience and literature to find a foothold in their understanding for the biblical message. Even then, Paul didn't begin with the gospel. He first laid a foundation with the understanding of God as Creator (Read Acts 17:24 in your Bible).

What was Paul's argument? _____

_____

_____

_____

He then argued that his listeners ought to understand for themselves that this God could not be like a silver idol. For if He created them, then He must be a personal Being. And hence, He was someone to whom they owed a personal allegiance—and someone to whom they were personally accountable. Only after establishing who God is and why we are morally responsible to Him did Paul talk about salvation and Jesus' resurrection.

How did Western culture in the first half of this century resemble the first-century Jewish culture?_____

_____

Did you include the following response in your answer: "Most students knew the Scriptures, even if they weren't always obedient to its commands."

Likewise, most American students had some sort of church affiliation and knew the basic tenets of Christianity, even if they went to church only on Easter. But that is no longer the case. Today, many students are completely unfamiliar with even basic biblical teaching, and we must find ways to engage people who think more like Greeks than Jews. We must follow the New Testament pattern for addressing a non-Christian culture. We are called to love people enough to reach out to them in their own language.

In ministering to a non-Christian culture, how are we to reach out to them? _____

_____

_____

_____

It is urgent that we understand Christianity as a worldview, not only for pre-evangelism, but also for apologetics. (Read 1 Peter 3:15). What reasons do you have for the hope in your life? _____

_____

_____

_____

The word *answer* comes from the Greek word *apologia*, meaning a defense, from which we get our word *apologetics*, meaning a defense or vindication of what we believe.

The world can accept that we love Jesus— they can even acknowledge the social benefits of religion—and still believe that He is merely a human or mythical figure. We need to offer reasons for belief. While it is true that no one comes to God apart from faith, Christianity is not an irrational leap. Examined objectively, it is a rational proposition that is well supported by reason and evidence. In fact, as we will argue through-

out this book, all other explanations of reality are irrational. J. Gresham Machen, one of the great fundamentalist theologians in the early part of this century, said that the purpose of apologetics is to "mold the thought of the world in such a way as to make the acceptance of Christianity something more than a logical absurdity."

Rewrite Machen's quote in your own words.

_____

_____

_____

_____

_____

But can we really persuade others, you might ask, in a culture so hostile and hardened? Yes, indeed, for we have a marvelous case to make, and people will listen if we cast it in terms of the questions they have.

The task of apologetics is not just for Christian pastors or intellectuals. God has created each of us with a mind, with the capacity to study, think, and ask questions. No one is an expert in every area, but each of us can master the subjects in which we have some experience.

Identify two subject areas you feel you have some experience talking about.

1. _____

_____

2. _____

_____

If our culture is to be transformed, it will happen from the bottom up—from ordinary believers, practicing apologetics at the Student Center, in the classroom, in the library, in the Greek house, or in the dorm. And let us always bear in mind the final words of Peter's admonition.

Read 1 Peter 3:15. How are believers to respond to a lost world?

1. _____

_____

> *People will listen if we cast it in terms of the questions they have.*

2. _____
_____
_____

Understanding Christianity as a worldview is important not just to fulfill the Great Commission but also to fulfill the cultural commission—the call to create a culture under the lordship of Christ. God cares not only about redeeming souls but also about restoring His creation. He calls us to be agents not only of His saving grace but also of His common grace. Our job is not only to build up the church but also to build a society to the glory of God.

God cares not only about _____ souls but also about _____ His creation. He calls us to be agents not only of His _____ grace, but also of His _____ grace. Our job is not only to build up the _____ but also to build a _____ to the _____ of God.

God's Word is sufficient for salvation—for saving grace. But here we are talking about common grace—that is, carrying out God's work of maintaining creation by promoting righteousness and restraining evil. To do this, we must translate God's revelation into the language of the world. We must be able to speak to the scientist in the language of science, to the artist in the language of art, to the politician in the language of politics.

How are you translating God's revelation into the language of your world? (Circle the appropriate number response for each of your "worlds.")

1	2	3	4	5	6	7	8	9	10

NOT SO GOOD   SO-SO   PRETTY WELL

The greatest commandment according to Jesus is, "Love the Lord your God with all your heart and with all your soul and with all your mind" (Matt. 22:37). Loving the Lord with your mind means understanding God's ordinances for all of creation, for the natural world, for societies, for businesses, for schools, for the government, for science and the arts.

What does Paul tell us to do with our thoughts? (Read 2 Corinthians 10:5 in your Bible). _____
_____
_____
_____

What does Paul tell us to do with our bodies? (Read Romans 12:1-2). _____
_____
_____
_____

Sadly, many Christians have been misled into believing there is a dichotomy between faith and reason, and as a result they have actually shunned intellectual pursuits. We must break down this false dichotomy between the spiritual and the intellectual and recover the calling to save minds—especially in our highly educated society. Unlike a generation ago, churches today are filled with college graduates; in fact, polls show that evangelicals are better educated than the general populace, a striking change from forty years ago. Pastors must begin to redefine their task to include **intellectual evangelism**, for if they do not preach to issues of the mind, they will find themselves increasingly alienated from their own flock.

Think for a moment about discussing "intellectual evangelism" with your pastor. How would you describe this concept to him? ____
_____
_____
_____

This is not a burdensome task, one more thing to whip ourselves into doing. I have found that developing a Christian mind is a rewarding and enriching act of discipleship. Back when I was in college, I was a moderately good student, at least in subjects I enjoyed, like history and political philosophy. But studying was work for me, even drudgery at times, particularly when it conflicted with fraternity parties. In law school, I was at the top of my class, but rarely because of genuine intellectual curiosity; I simply wanted to be the best at my profession.

But after my conversion to Christianity, I felt a keen desire to learn about God's work throughout history.

History and literature and science all took on new meaning because I began to see these disciplines as explorations of God's truth. It was exciting to be able to see through all the pretensions of the philosophies I had studied in college. It was as if a searchlight were shone into a cave, exposing the dark holes and crevices.

My intellectual curiosity has not abated. When I read about the history of modern liberalism, for example, or Renaissance art or ancient understandings of law, I am not merely absorbing knowledge for its own sake. I am understanding God's creative handiwork. I am witnessing God's great morality drama that we call human history. *And I am learning how to defend God's truth better.*

In what ways can God's truth be revealed in the courses you are taking? _____
_____
_____
_____

Dare we believe that Christianity can yet prevail? We must believe it. This is an historic moment of opportunity, and when the church is faithful to its calling, it always leads to a reformation of culture. When the church is truly the church, a community living in biblical obedience and contending for their faith in every area of life, it will surely revive the surrounding culture, or create a new one.

Turn to Romans 12:1-2 and answer the following questions.

What does Paul encourage us to do? (v. 1) ___
_____
_____
_____

How can a Christian be a living sacrifice? (v. 1) _____
_____
_____

What is meant by "holy and acceptable"? (v. 1) (Check a Bible commentary for your response.) _____
_____
_____

What are we instructed not to do? (v. 2) ____
_____
_____

What are we instructed to do? (v. 2) _____
_____
_____

What is meant by good, acceptable, and perfect? (v. 2) _____
_____
_____

✔ Points to Remember
List two key points of today's session.
1. _____
_____
2. _____
_____

❓ Questions to Ask
What questions do I have concerning what I've read today? _____
_____
_____
_____
_____
_____

Actions to Take

Based on what I've read, what specific action(s) should I take? _____

_____

_____

_____

Prayers to Pray

Today, God, you taught me _____

_____

_____

_____

_____

_____

Help me, Lord, to _____

_____

_____

_____

_____

_____

_____

_____

DAY FIVE

Finding the Beginning

"I am not ashamed of the gospel, because it is the power of God for the salvation of everyone who believes: first for the Jew, then for the Gentile" (Romans 1:16).

Every worldview has to begin somewhere, has to begin with a theory of how the universe began. Naturalism begins with the fundamental assumption that the forces of nature alone are adequate to explain everything that exists. Whereas the Bible says, "In the beginning was the Word" (John 1:1), naturalism says that in the beginning were the particles, along with blind, purposeless natural laws. Naturalism says that nature is our creator.

Genesis 1:1 says that _____ is our

_____.

Naturalistic scientists try to give the impression that they are fair-minded and objective, implying that religious people are subjective, biased in favor of their personal beliefs. But this is a ruse, for naturalism is as much a philosophy, a worldview, a personal belief system as any religion is.

Naturalism begins with certain premises that cannot be tested empirically. One premise is that nature is "all that is or ever was or ever will be," to use a line from the late Carl Sagan's popular science program "Cosmos." This is not a scientific statement, for there is no conceivable way it could be tested. It is a philosophy that supports the entire evolutionary enterprise, from its assertions about the beginning of the universe to the beginning of life to the appearance of complex life forms.

Identify two statements you just read which describe what naturalism tries to do.

1. _____

_____

2. _____

_____

As much as anyone else, it was the late Carl Sagan who popularized the naturalistic worldview and entrenched it firmly in the minds of the average American. His dark hair swept to one side, the Colgate smile, the telegenic personality—it all added up to a powerful influence on the millions of viewers who tuned in to his PBS program "Cosmos." Week after week, he brought stunning images of exploding stars and sprawling nebula into homes and classrooms across the nation.

But that's not all Sagan brought. With his engaging manner, he was a televangelist for naturalism, a philosophy he held with all the fervor of a religion. And logically so, for whatever you take as the starting point of your worldview does function, in effect, as your religion.

Consider these seven statements by Sagan. Under each statement identify a Scripture reference and a brief summary of the Scripture which contradicts Sagan's worldview and identifies God's ultimate truth. You may need to do this with a Christian friend.

1. "The Cosmos is all that is or ever was or ever will be."
Scripture: _____
Truth:_____

2. Sagan mockingly described the Christian God as "an outsized, light-skinned male with a long white beard, sitting on a throne somewhere up there in the sky, busily tallying the fall of every sparrow."
Scripture: _____
Truth:_____

3. Sagan regarded the Cosmos as the only self-existing, eternal being: "A universe that is infinitely old requires no Creator."
Scripture: _____
Truth:_____
_____

4. Sagan says that, "We are, in the most profound sense, children of the Cosmos," for it is the Cosmos that gave us birth and daily sustains us.

Scripture: _____
Truth:_____
_____

5. Sagan hints that the astronomer's urge to explore the Cosmos is motivated by a mystical recognition that the chemicals in our bodies were originally forged in space—that outer space is our origin and our true home: "Some part of our being knows this is from where we came. We long to return."
Scripture: _____
Truth:_____
_____

6. Sagan's worship of the Cosmos prescribes certain moral duties for its adherents. "Our matter, our form, and much of our character is determined by the deep connection between life and the Cosmos."
Scripture: _____
Truth:_____
_____

7. Sagan's worship of the Cosmos even tells us how to be saved. Threats to human survival—pollution, war, food shortages—have nothing to do with moral failings. Instead, they result from technological incompetence.
Scripture: _____
Truth:_____
_____

Is there any more poignant example of why Christian college students need to learn how to argue persuasively against naturalism? It is pressed on our imagination long before we can think rationally and critically. It is presented everywhere as the only worldview supported by science. And it is diametrically opposed to Christianity.

Do you recall a time when you were taught naturalistic views? Briefly record what you remember below: _____
_____
_____
_____

**Carl Sagan
(1934-1996)**

Born Nov. 9, 1934, in Brooklyn, N.Y. , Carl Sagan is famous for his research on the origins of life and his belief that life exists elsewhere in the universe.
Sagan became a leading figure in the search for extraterrestrial intelligence with his involvement in the Mariner, Viking, and Voyager spacecraft expeditions to Venus and the outer planets.
Sagan passed away on December 20, 1996.

> *The real battle is worldview against worldview, religion against religion. On one side is the naturalistic worldview, claiming that the universe is the product of blind, purposeless forces. On the other side stands the Christian worldview, telling us we were created by a transcendent God who loves us and has a purpose for us.*

The Christian collegian must be ready, then, to separate genuine science from philosophy. Evolution, as it is typically presented in textbooks and museums, confuses the two; what most secular scientists label as "science" is actually their personal philosophy or religion. Science has come to be defined as naturalistic philosophy; the "scientific" answer is always the theory that appeals to natural forces alone.

The real battle is worldview against worldview, religion against religion. On one side is the naturalistic worldview, claiming that the universe is the product of blind, purposeless forces. On the other side stands the Christian worldview, telling us we were created by a transcendent God who loves us and has a purpose for us. Nature itself is covered with His "fingerprints," marks of purpose in every area of scientific investigation. Our case is fully defensible, if only we learn how to make it.

What does the naturalistic worldview proclaim? _____
_____
_____
_____

What does the Christian worldview proclaim? _____
_____
_____

The Christian worldview begins with creation, with a deliberate act by a personal Being who existed from all eternity. This personal dimension is crucial for understanding creation. Before bringing the world into existence, the Creator made a choice, a decision: He set out a plan, an intelligent design.

Take a moment now to thank God for His wonderful plan which includes you!

Turn to Romans 1:16-25 in your Bible and answer the following questions.

1. How are Christians to live their lives? (v. 17) _____
2. Who receives God's wrath? (v. 18) _____
3. Why are people without any excuse? (vv. 19-20) _____
4. How did the unrighteous respond to God? (v. 21) _____
5. What was God's response to the unrighteous? (v. 24) _____
6. What did the unrighteous exchange God for? (v. 25) _____

✅ Points to Remember
List two key points of today's session.
1. _____
_____
2. _____
_____

❓ Questions to Ask
What questions do I have concerning what I've read today? _____
_____
_____

👥 Actions to Take
Based on what I've read, what specific action(s) should I take? _____
_____
_____

✳ Prayers to Pray
Today, God, you taught me _____
_____
_____

Help me, Lord, to _____
_____
_____

Where Did I Come From?

Are you puzzled by the scientific explanation of how the world was created? This session will provide you with another set of glasses to use as we look at the creation of the world from a Biblical worldview.

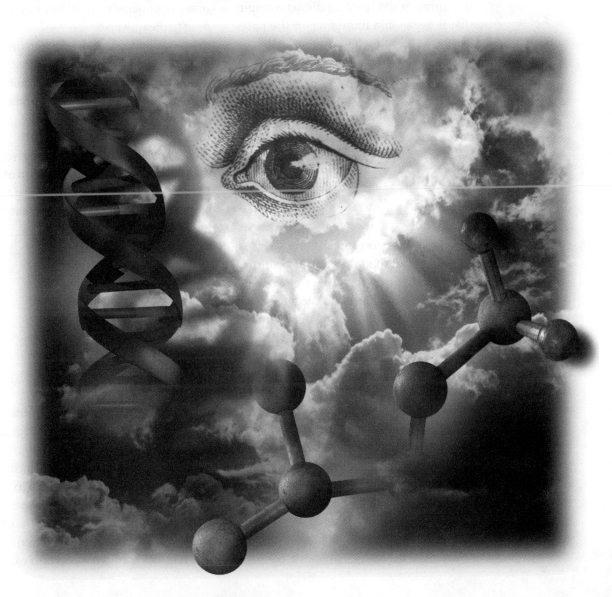

A Beginning to the Universe

"In the beginning God created the heavens and the earth" (Genesis 1:1).

The first question any worldview has to ask is how it all started. How did the universe begin? Where did it come from? After maintaining for centuries that the physical universe is eternal and therefore needs no Creator, science today has uncovered dramatic new evidence that the universe did have an ultimate origin, that it began at a finite time in the past—just as the Bible teaches.

Your philosophy professor has just asked you the question, "How did the universe begin?" How do you answer him?_____

_____

_____

_____

_____

_____

To grasp just how revolutionary this is, we must recall that most ancient cultures believed that the universe is eternal—or, more precisely, that it was formed from some kind of primordial material that is eternal. The ancient Greeks even argued that the idea of an ultimate beginning is rationally inconceivable. Their arguments were revived during the late Middle Ages and Renaissance, when classical literature was rediscovered. Then, in the eighteenth century, scientists formulated the law of conservation of matter (that matter can be neither created nor destroyed), and it became a potent weapon in the hands of ardent materialists, who argued that science itself now ruled out any ultimate creation.

Then, in the early twentieth century, several lines of evidence began a curious convergence: the implication from general relativity theory that the universe is expanding, the finding that the stars exhibit a "red shift," implying that they are moving outward, and finally, the realization that the two laws of thermodynamics actually make it imperative to believe in a beginning to the universe.

The second law of thermodynamics, the law of decay, implies that the universe is in a process of gradual disintegration—implacably moving toward final darkness and decay.

These various lines of evidence coalesced in the 1960s and led to the formulation of a Big Bang theory. From research or talking to a professor, write down a brief explanation of the Big Bang theory._____

_____

_____

_____

_____

_____

_____

_____

The new theory hit the scientific world like a thunderclap. *It meant that the idea of an ultimate beginning was no longer merely religious dogma.* Science itself now indicated that the universe burst into existence at a particular time in the remote past.

What's more, the first law of thermodynamics (the conservation of matter) implies that matter cannot just pop into existence

Explosive Evidence of Creation

Understanding the "Big Bang" has been one of the most exciting scientific developments of our century. Evidence from several areas of physics shows that the universe came into existence at a specific time in the past. Science now proves what the Bible has said all along—the universe had a beginning point. "In the beginning, God created…" (Gen. 1:1).

The Big Bang theory delivers a near-fatal blow to naturalistic philosophy, for the naturalistic credo regards reality as an unbroken sequence of cause and effect that can be traced back endlessly. But the Big Bang represents a sudden discontinuity in the chain of cause and effect.

or create itself. Thus if the universe had a beginning, then something external to the universe must have caused it to come into existence—something, or Someone, transcendent to the natural world. As a result, the idea of creation is no longer merely a matter of religious faith; it is a conclusion based on the most straightforward reading of the scientific evidence.

The Big Bang theory delivers a near-fatal blow to naturalistic philosophy, for the naturalistic credo regards reality as an unbroken sequence of cause and effect that can be traced back endlessly. But the Big Bang represents a sudden discontinuity in the chain of cause and effect. It means science can trace events back in time only to a certain point; at the moment of the Big Bang explosion, science reaches an abrupt break, an absolute barrier.

Share briefly how the Big Bang theory affected naturalistic philosophy and why.

_____
_____
_____
_____
_____
_____
_____
_____

Naturalists have no way to avoid the challenge posed by the Big Bang theory without twisting themselves into impossible logical contortions. The facts clearly indicate that the universe is not eternal, that it cannot originate itself; therefore, the implication is that the universe began suddenly and sharply, at a definite moment in time, in a flash of light and energy.

What is the implication of the Big Bang theory? _____
_____
_____
_____

What came before the Big Bang? What caused it? If the Big Bang was the origin of the universe itself, then its cause must be something outside the universe. The truth is that the Big Bang theory gives dramatic support to the biblical teaching that the universe had an ultimate beginning—that space, matter, and time itself are finite.

What support does the Big Bang theory give to biblical teaching? _____
_____
_____
_____

After the first spacecraft landed on the moon, one stunning photograph quickly became familiar to all Americans: a view of the cloud-wrapped Earth, seen just above the horizon of the black and cratered surface of the moon. The contrast was striking. Our beautiful blue and white planet, so hospitable to life, seen against the stark, barren, lifeless lunar landscape.

From the perspective of the space age, it has become clearer than ever that Earth is unique. It boasts a wealth of characteristics that make it capable of supporting life—a nearly endless list of preconditions that have been exquisitely met only, as far as we know, on our planet.

How does Earth happen to be so special? Is it just coincidence? Luck? Or was it designed by a loving Creator who had us in mind from the outset?

What are some examples of how our Earth is so special? _____
_____
_____
_____

Consider the structure of the atom. Everything in the universe is made of atoms, from the stars in the farthest heavens to the cells in your body—and the atom itself is a bundle of fortuitous "coincidences." Within the atom, the neutron is just slightly more massive than the proton, which means that free neutrons (those not trapped within an atom) can decay and turn into protons. If things were reversed—if it were the proton that was larger and had a tendency to decay—the very structure of the universe would be impossible.

Why? Because a free proton is simply a hydrogen atom, and if free protons had a tendency to decay, then everything made of hydrogen would decay. The sun, which is made of hydrogen, would melt away. Water, a liquid oxide of hydrogen (H_2O) would be impossible. In fact, the universe itself would decay, since about 74 percent of the observed universe consists of hydrogen.

The list of "coincidences" goes on and on. It turns out that the slightest tinkering with the values of the fundamental forces of physics—gravity, electromagnetism, the strong and weak nuclear forces—would have resulted in a universe where life is utterly impossible. The anthropic principle states that in our own universe, all of these seemingly arbitrary and unrelated values in physics have one strange thing in common: they are precisely the values needed to get a universe capable of supporting life.

If the universe exhibits design, it is logical to conclude that there is a Designer. The most obvious inference is that the universe appears to be designed because it is designed—powerful evidence for the biblical worldview that a loving God created the world.

Turn to Genesis 1 in the Old Testament of your Bible and answer the following questions.
1. What one fact is stated in verse 1? _____
_____

The Atom

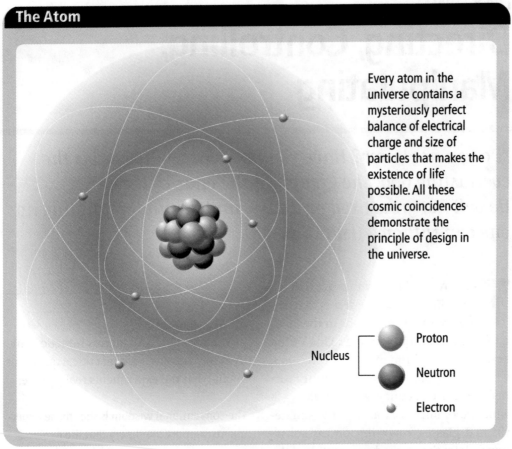

Every atom in the universe contains a mysteriously perfect balance of electrical charge and size of particles that makes the existence of life possible. All these cosmic coincidences demonstrate the principle of design in the universe.

Nucleus — Proton
Neutron

Electron

2. Identify each part of God's creation and its function.

GOD CREATED... IN ORDER TO...

Day One _____

Day Two _____

Day Three _____

Day Four _____

Day Five _____

Day Six _____

✔ Points to Remember
List two key points of today's session.

1. _____
_____

2. _____
_____

❓ Questions to Ask
What questions do I have concerning what I've read today? _____
_____
_____
_____

👥 Actions to Take
Based on what I've read, what specific action(s) should I take? _____
_____
_____
_____
_____
_____

✳ Prayers to Pray
Today, God, you taught me _____
_____
_____
_____
_____

Help me, Lord, to _____
_____
_____
_____
_____

Where Did I Come From?

DAY TWO
Directing, Controlling, Manipulating

"Do you not know? Have you not heard? The Lord is the everlasting God, the Creator of the ends of the earth. He will not grow tired or weary, and his understanding no one can fathom" (Isaiah 40:28).

The way scientists try to prove that life arose in the primitive seas is to recreate the same conditions in the laboratory and see what happens. One of the best-known experiments began in 1953, when newspapers across the country carried photos of Stanley Miller wearing a white laboratory coat and heavy square-rimmed glasses, reporting on his sensational claim that he had accomplished the first step toward creating life in a test tube.

Miller had mixed simple chemicals and gases in a glass tube, then zapped them with an electrical charge to induce chemical reactions. The idea was to simulate conditions on the early earth and show that simple chemicals could indeed react to create the building blocks of life. To everyone's surprise, what emerged at the other end of the laboratory apparatus were amino acids, the building blocks of protein, an important constituent of living things. The news was electrifying. Few people had dared dream that the elements of a living cell could be produced by a completely natural, random process. Miller's success seemed to provide dramatic evidence for a naturalistic account of life's origin.

Have scientists created life in a test tube? How would you answer this question and why? Write down your answer below.

_____

The problem with all this frenetic activity is that no one is asking critical questions about what the experiments really prove.

The conventional wisdom is that these experiments support the theory that life evolved spontaneously from simple chemicals in a primeval pond about four billion years ago. But do they? ❑ Yes ❑ No

Why or why not, in your opinion? _____
_____
_____
_____
_____

Let's start with the amino acids that came out of Miller's test tube. The truth is that these differ in critical ways from those found in living things. Amino acids come in two forms, what scientists call left-handed and right-handed. Living things are highly selective: They use only the left-handed form. But when Miller and his colleagues mixed chemicals in the laboratory, they got both kinds—an even fifty-fifty mix of left-handed and right-handed. In fact, this is what happens every time anyone mixes the chemicals randomly in the laboratory. There is no natural process that produces only left-handed amino acids, the kind required by living things. All of this means that the amino acids formed in the test tube are useless for life.

And that's only the first problem. The next step to "creating life" is to get amino acids to link up and form proteins. The proteins in living things are comprised of amino acids hooked together in a very particular chemical bond called a peptide bond. But amino acids are like Tinkertoys: They're capable of hooking together in all sorts of different ways, forming several different chemical bonds. And in the test tube, that's exactly what they do. They hook up in a variety of ways, never producing a genuine protein that could function in a living cell.

In addition, for a protein to be functional, the amino acids must link up in a particular sequence, just like the sequence of letters in a sentence. If you scramble the letters in a sentence, you get nonsense; if you scramble the amino acids in a protein, you get a nonfunctional protein. Yet in laboratory experiments, all we get are scrambled, random sequences. There's no natural force capable of selecting the right amino acids and lining them up in the right order. As a result, the protein-like chains that appear in the test tube are useless for life.

The fact is, the much-touted experiments tell us nothing about where real, functional proteins came from. Yet this inconvenient fact is rarely mentioned when headlines blare out the news that scientists have succeeded in creating the building blocks of life.

In your own words, summarize this "inconvenient fact." _____
_____
_____
_____
_____
_____

Someone has just asked you the question, "Have scientists created life in a test tube?" Write down your response. _____
_____
_____
_____
_____

At every turn, the experiments that have ignited so much excitement turn out to be artificial. As a result, even the most successful origin-of-life experiments tell us nothing about what could have happened under natural conditions. They tell us only what happens when a brilliant scientist manipulates the conditions, "coaxing" the materials down the chemical pathways necessary to produce the building blocks of life.

So what do these experiments really prove? Share your answer to this question in the space below. _____
_____
_____
_____
_____
_____

These experiments prove that *life can be created only by an intelligent agent directing, controlling, and manipulating the process.* The latest scientific findings do not discredit biblical faith; rather, they provide positive evidence that the origin of life requires an intelligent agent, a creator.

If we need additional confirmation, it is coming from a surprising place: from the use of computers in biology. Long before the information age, the living cell was thought to be quite simple, and it was easy enough to think life arose by chance. But as science began uncovering the marvelous complexity of the cell, it became harder and harder to hold on to chance theories.

Biologists took refuge in the idea of nearly endless time. Given enough time,

At every turn, the experiments that have ignited so much excitement turn out to be artificial.

These experiments prove that life can be created only by an intelligent agent directing, controlling, and manipulating the process. The latest scientific findings do not discredit biblical faith; rather, they provide positive evidence that the origin of life requires an intelligent agent, a creator.

The Complexity of a Cell

April 12, 1999: A computer model of a cell requires a minimum of 127 genes.
A group led by biologist and computer scientist Masaru Tomita at Keio University in Fujisawa, Japan, has built a computer model of a cell. The "bare-bones" model, called "E-CELL," requires 127 genes, the minimum needed to model a cell, they find.[1]

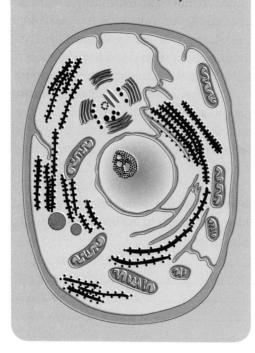

they argued, anything can happen. Over millions of years, the unlikely becomes likely, the improbable is transformed into the inevitable.

But the computer revolution put an end to any chance theory of life's origin. Beginning in the 1960s, mathematicians began writing computer programs to simulate every process under the sun, and they cast their calculating eyes on evolution itself. The outcome was jolting: The computers showed that the probability that life arose by chance is essentially zero, no matter how long the time scale.

What have we learned from computers in biology? _____
_____
_____

As a result, today it is common to hear prominent scientists scoff at the idea that life arose by chance. Yet it is becoming ever clearer that the experiments fail to support any naturalistic theory of life's origin. What they do support is the idea of intelligent design. The experiments give positive evidence that life arises only when the raw materials are carefully selected, arranged, and organized and only when the process is guided, controlled, manipulated, and pointed in the right direction.

The advance of science is not casting up new challenges to Christian faith, as we are so often told. Instead, it is uncovering ever more powerful evidence that what Christians believe is true on all levels, including the natural world. And that is becoming even more true today as scientists learn more about what is inside the cell—and especially the structure of DNA.

We've all heard the term DNA. Simply put, DNA is like a language in the heart of the cell, a molecular message, and it contains a staggering amount of information. A single cell of the human body contains as much information as the *Encyclopedia Britannica*—all thirty volumes—three or four times over. As a result, the question of the origin of life must now be redefined as the question of the origin of biological information.

From what you have read up to this point, give a response to these two questions:

1. Can "information" arise by natural forces alone? _____
_____
_____
_____
_____

2. Does it require an intelligent agent?
❏ Yes ❏ No   Why or why not? _____
_____
_____
_____

Scientists committed to naturalism must try to construct an explanation of life based solely on physical-chemical laws. They must explain the information in DNA as a product of natural processes at work in the chemicals that comprise living things.

It's true that DNA is composed of ordinary chemicals (bases, sugars, phosphates) that react according to ordinary laws. But what makes DNA function as a message is not the chemicals themselves but rather their sequence, their pattern. The chemicals in DNA are grouped into molecules (called nucleotides) that act like letters in a message, and they must be in a particular order if the message is going to be intelligible. If the letters are scrambled, the result is nonsense.

Since DNA is a message, the case can be stated even more strongly in terms of *information theory*, a field of research that investigates the ways information is transmitted. As we said earlier, the naturalistic scientist has only two possible ways to explain the origin of life—either chance or natural law. But information theory gives us a powerful tool for discounting both these explanations, for both chance and law lead to structures with low information content, whereas DNA has a very high information content.

A structure or message is said to have high or low information content depending on the minimum number of instructions needed to tell you how to construct it. To illustrate, a random sequence of letters has low information content because it requires only two instructions: (1) select a letter of the English alphabet and write it down, and (2) do it again (select another letter and write it down). By that token, a regular, repetitive pattern of letters has low information content as well.

In nature, both random patterns and regular patterns (like ripples on a beach) have low information content. By contrast, DNA has a very high information content. It would be impossible to produce a simple

DNA: The Thread of Life

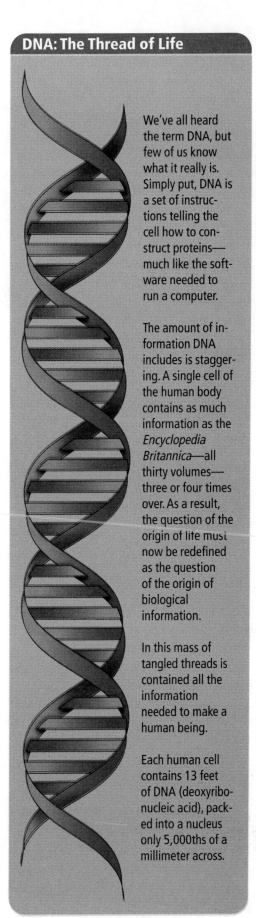

We've all heard the term DNA, but few of us know what it really is. Simply put, DNA is a set of instructions telling the cell how to construct proteins—much like the software needed to run a computer.

The amount of information DNA includes is staggering. A single cell of the human body contains as much information as the *Encyclopedia Britannica*—all thirty volumes—three or four times over. As a result, the question of the origin of life must now be redefined as the question of the origin of biological information.

In this mass of tangled threads is contained all the information needed to make a human being.

Each human cell contains 13 feet of DNA (deoxyribonucleic acid), packed into a nucleus only 5,000ths of a millimeter across.

DNA has a completely different structure from any other thing that can be explained by either chance or natural law, and information theory gives us the conceptual tools to debunk any such attempts to explain the origin of life.

When it comes to the origin of life, science is squarely on the side of creation by an intelligent agent. We have nothing to fear from the progress of science.

set of instructions telling a chemist how to synthesize the DNA of even the simplest bacterium. You would have to specify every chemical "letter," one by one—and there are literally millions. Thus DNA has a completely different structure from any other thing that can be explained by either chance or natural law, and information theory gives us the conceptual tools to debunk any such attempts to explain the origin of life.

Another attempt to find a naturalistic answer to the origin of life comes from the new field of *complexity theory*. On their computer screens, researchers "grow" marvelous shapes that resemble ferns and forests and snowflakes, and then these researchers claim that they have finally found the answer to the question of spontaneous order.

Is this new field of research finally going to uncover a law that can account for the spontaneous origin of life itself? What do you think? Check one and explain your answer.

❑ Yes ❑ No _____

_____

_____

_____

The verdict is already in, and the answer is no. The conclusion is that there are no known physical laws capable of creating a structure like DNA with a high information content. Based on both the latest scientific knowledge and on ordinary experience, we know only one cause that is up to the task: an intelligent agent. Only an intelligent **Being** could create the DNA molecule.

Information theory makes it clear that natural forces do not produce structures with high information content. This is not a statement about our ignorance—a "gap" in knowledge that will be filled in later by a natural explanation. Rather, it is a statement about what we know—about our consistent experience of the character of natural processes. Today, holding on to the

hope that some natural process will be found to explain DNA is supremely irrational. The elusive process that naturalists hope to find would have to be completely unprecedented, different in kind from any we currently know. Surely this is an argument from ignorance.

When it comes to the origin of life, science is squarely on the side of creation by an intelligent agent. We have nothing to fear from the progress of science.

Turn to Isaiah 40:18-31 in your Old Testament and answer the following questions.

1. What is Isaiah asking in verse 21? _____

_____

_____

2. According to verse 26, what has God done?

_____

_____

_____

3. How can we "wait upon the Lord"? _____

_____

_____

_____

✅ Points to Remember
List two key points of today's session.

1. _____

_____

2. _____

_____

❓ Questions to Ask
What questions do I have concerning what I've read today? _____

_____

_____

_____

🛠 Actions to Take
Based on what I've read, what specific action(s) should I take? _____

_____

_____

_____

Prayers to Pray

Today, God, you taught me _____

_____
_____
_____
_____
_____
_____
_____
_____

Help me, Lord, to _____

_____
_____
_____
_____
_____
_____
_____

DAY THREE

Organisms Stay True to Type

"And whatever you do, whether in word or deed, do it all in the name of the Lord Jesus, giving thanks to God the Father through him" (Colossians 3:17).

Consider this typical example, from the widely used college textbook *Evolutionary Biology*: "By coupling undirected, purposeless variation to the blind, uncaring process of natural selection, Darwin made theological or spiritual explanations of the life processes superfluous."[2]

We must all know how to respond to the challenge posed by Darwinian naturalism. Fortunately, a few basic concepts will help us cut through the rhetoric and enable us to think more clearly. The best argument against Darwinism has been known for centuries by farmers and breeders, and it can be stated in a simple principle: Natural change in living things is limited. Or, stated positively: **Organisms stay true to type.**

Remember Darwin, perhaps from an earlier class in high school? Write below what you remember to be the main message of Darwin. _____

_____

Darwinism cannot deny that all observed change is limited, but what the theory does suggest is that over time these minor variations add up to create major changes—the vast changes necessary to go from a primeval one-celled organism to bees and butterflies and little boys. This is the core of Darwinian theory—yet, ironically, it is also the easiest part of the theory to discredit. Even Charles Darwin's own work breeding pigeons demonstrates the limits of biological change.

In Victorian England, pigeon breeding was extremely popular, and when Darwin returned from his famous sea voyage to the Galapagos Islands, he took up pigeon breeding. In the skillful hands of a breeder, the pigeon can be transformed into a Chinese fantail, with stunning tail feathers; it can become a pouter, with a huge crop bulging under its beak; it can become a Jacobin, with a "hood" of feathers on the back and sides of its head resembling the hoods worn by Jacobin monks. Yet despite

this range of diversity, all pigeons are descendants of the common rock pigeon, the ordinary gray birds that flock in our city parks. And despite the spectacular variation in tails and feathers, all the pigeons Darwin observed remained pigeons. They never even divided into separate species.

What do you think is Darwin's flaw? Write your thoughts here. _____
_____
_____
_____
_____

Here's the fatal flaw in Darwin's theory: Centuries of experiments show that the change produced by breeding does not continue at a steady rate from generation to generation. Instead, change is rapid at first, then levels off, and eventually reaches a ceiling that breeders cannot cross.

Despite what the textbooks say, Darwin did not prove that nature is capable of crossing those "fixed limitations." He suggested only that it was theoretically possible—that minor changes might have accumulated over thousands of years until a fish became an amphibian, an amphibian became a reptile, and a reptile became a mammal. But after more than 150 years, it has become clear that Darwin's speculation flies in the face of all the results of breeding and laboratory experimentation.

The simple words from the first chapter of Genesis still stand firm: And God made every living thing to reproduce (fill-in-the-blanks) _____ _____ _____ _____ "
(see Genesis 1: 11-12, 21, 24-25).

Darwinism and Neo-Darwinism

Due to modern discoveries in the fields of microbiology and genetics, Darwin's original theory has been thoroughly scientifically discredited. In fact, natural selection serves to prevent evolution by screening out changes. Darwinism has been replaced by neo (new) darwinism, which considers genetic mutations as the source of evolutionary change. We have chosen to use darwinism consistently through this study to refer to the original theory, its newer form, and all evolution, though we recognize that the theory predates Darwin.

The great Christian evangelist Francis Schaeffer offers an argument against evolution that is simple, easy to grasp, and devastating: Suppose a fish evolves lungs. What happens then? Does it move up to the next evolutionary stage?

Of course not. It drowns.

Living things cannot simply change piecemeal—a new organ here, a new limb there. An organism is an integrated system, and any isolated change in the system is more likely to be harmful than helpful. If a fish's gills were to begin mutating into a set of lungs, that would not be an advantage; it would be a disaster. The only way to turn a fish into a land-dwelling animal is to transform it all at once, with a host of interrelated changes happening at the same time—not only lungs but also coadapted changes in the skeleton, the circulatory system, and so on.

The term to describe this kind of interdependent system is *irreducible complexity*. And the fact that organisms are irreducibly complex is yet another argument that they could not have evolved piecemeal, one step at a time, as Darwin proposed. Darwinian theory states that all living structures evolved in small, gradual steps from simpler structures—feathers from scales, wings from forelegs, blossoms from leaves, and so on. But anything that is irreducibly complex cannot evolve in gradual steps, and thus its very existence refutes Darwin's theory.

In your opinion, how does "irreducible complexity" argue against Darwin's theory? _____
_____
_____
_____
_____

On all fronts, scientists are being forced to face up to the implications of an intelligent cause. Science cannot tell us everything we might wish to know about this intelligent cause, of course. Biology cannot reveal who the Creator is, and it cannot explain God's plan of salvation. These are tasks for theology. But a study of the design and purpose in nature does clearly reveal God's existence—so clearly that, as the apostle Paul writes in the New Testament, we stand before Him without excuse.

Read in the New Testament, Romans 1:20. Why are we "without excuse"? _____
_____
_____

If the scientific evidence is so persuasive, why do you feel the scientific establishment clings so tenaciously to Darwinian evolution?
_____
_____
_____
_____

The real issue is not what we see through the microscope or the telescope; it's what we hold in our hearts and minds.

Every worldview has to begin somewhere—God or matter, take your choice. Then everything else flows from that initial choice. This is why the question of creation has become such a fierce battleground today. It is the foundation of the entire Christian worldview. If God created all of finite reality, then every aspect of that reality must be subject to Him and His truth. Everything finds its meaning and interpretation in relation to God. No part of life can be autonomous or neutral, no part can be sliced off and made independent from Christian truth. Because creation includes the whole scope of finite reality, the Christian worldview must be equally comprehensive, covering every aspect of our lives, our thinking, our choices. Both friends and foes of Christianity realize that everything stands or falls on the doctrine of creation.

Christians on campus often seek to evangelize non-Christians by starting with the message of salvation—John 3:16 and

The fact that organisms are irreducibly complex is yet another argument that they could not have evolved piecemeal, one step at a time, as Darwin proposed.

Every worldview has to begin somewhere—God or matter, take your choice. Then everything else flows from that initial choice. This is why the question of creation has become such a fierce battleground today. It is the foundation of the entire Christian worldview.

Christianity is not merely a religion, defined narrowly as personal piety and corporate worship. It is an objective perspective on all of reality, a complete worldview. And when it comes to submitting worldviews to the test of practical living, only Christianity consistently works.

the rest of it. And for an earlier generation, that approach worked. Most people had some kind of church experience in their background, even if they did not believe the gospel message. But in today's post-Christian world, many people no longer even understand the meaning of crucial biblical terms. For example, the basic term "sin" makes no sense to people if they have no concept of a holy God who created us and who therefore has a right to require certain things of us. If people don't understand sin, they certainly don't comprehend the need for salvation.

What does the Bible say about our sin and our need for salvation? (The book of Romans offers some ideas.)

Romans 3:23 _____

Romans 5:6 _____

Romans 5:8 _____

Romans 6:23 _____

The Scientific Case for Creation and Design Is Powerful.

1. Cosmology has discovered the shattering truth that matter is not eternal after all, as naturalistic scientists once confidently assumed. It began at a finite period of time—which in turn implies that something outside the universe must have set it going.

2. There are the staggering "coincidences" that make the universe fit for life. From the molecular properties of water to the balance of electrical charges in the proton and electron, the entire structure of the physical universe is exquisitely designed to support life on Earth.

3. Laboratory experiments touted as proof that life can arise spontaneously by random natural forces turn out to prove nothing of the sort. Instead, they provide positive evidence that life can be created only by an intelligent agent controlling, directing, and manipulating the process. The discovery of DNA gives explosive new force to the argument for design. If

we rely on experience—and, after all, science is supposed to be based on experience—the only known source of information is an intelligent cause.

4. Once life appeared, Darwin did not succeed in demonstrating that it developed by mindless, undirected natural forces. Experiments with breeding and mutations have shown that his fundamental assumption—that living things can vary endlessly—is fatally flawed. Today, the most advanced investigations into the heart of the cell confirm that the irreducible complexity of living things can be explained only by intelligent design.

The continued dominance of Darwinism has less to do with its scientific validity than with a commitment to naturalism. Naturalism, in turn, has spread like a toxic oil spill into fields as diverse as ethics, law, education, and postmodernism—to name just a few. Thus Darwinism has become the cornerstone for a comprehensive philosophy in stark opposition to Christianity.

List four reasons why science makes a case for creation:

1. _____

_____

2. _____

_____

3. _____

_____

4. _____

_____

Christianity is not merely a religion, defined narrowly as personal piety and corporate worship. It is an objective perspective on all of reality, a complete worldview. And when it comes to submitting worldviews to the test of practical living, only Christianity consistently works. Only Christianity gives us an accurate road map; only Christianity matches the way we must act, if we are to live humanely and rationally in the real world.

Turn in the New Testament to Colossians 3:1-17 and answer the following questions.

1. What do verses 1 and 2 say about our "affection"? _____
_____
_____
_____

2. What are Christians to "put off"? _____
_____
_____
_____

3. What are Christians to "put on"? _____
_____
_____
_____

4. Read and rewrite verse 17 in your own words. _____
_____
_____
_____

✔ Points to Remember

List two key points of today's session.

1. _____
_____

2. _____
_____

❓ Questions to Ask

What questions do I have concerning what I've read today? _____
_____
_____
_____

🧑 Actions to Take

Based on what I've read, what specific action(s) should I take? _____
_____
_____
_____

✳ Prayers to Pray

Today, God, you taught me _____
_____
_____
_____
_____

Help me, Lord, to _____
_____
_____
_____
_____

DAY FOUR

Four Questions of Orgin

"Before I formed you in the womb I knew you, before you were born I set you apart; I appointed you as a prophet to the nations" (Jeremiah 1:5).

The most vexing cultural issues of our day—abortion, assisted suicide, euthanasia, genetic engineering—all turn on questions about what it means to be human, the value of human life, and how life should be protected, which, in turn, center on the question of our origin.

Four Questions of Origin

1. What is the meaning of human existence?
2. Where did we come from?
3. Why are we here?
4. What is the value of human life?

Christians believe that God created

human beings in His own image. And because human life bears this divine stamp, life is sacred, a gift from the Creator. He and He alone can set the boundaries of when we live and when we die. Against this, as we saw in earlier chapters, is the naturalistic belief that life arose from the primordial sea in a chance collision of chemicals, and through billions of years of chance mutations, this biological accident gave rise to the first humans. Millions of people today accept this basic presupposition that we are little more than grown-up germs.

These two worldviews are antithetical, and this antithesis lies at the very heart of our present cultural crisis. The question of where life comes from is not some academic argument for scientists to debate. Our understanding of the origin of life is intensely personal. It determines what we believe about human identity, what we value, and what we believe is the very reason for living. It determines who lives and who dies. This is why ethical questions surrounding human life have become the great defining debate of our age.

List two ways you have you noticed the questions on human life being debated today.
1. _____
_____
2. _____
_____

The shift from a culture of life to a culture of death has been like a shift in the tectonic plates underlying the continents—as sudden as an earthquake, when measured against the long view of history. It occurred largely in the 1960s, although as with so much else in American life, the fault lines were evident centuries earlier, in the Age of Reason and the Enlightenment.

The death of God means the death of morality. This logic was pressed by a decidedly odd prophet—Friedrich Nietzsche, a German who peered into the soul of our

century and later went insane. "Whither is God?" Nietzsche asked in 1889. "I will tell you, we have killed him—you and I. All of us are his murderers!"[3] He was incensed that the majority of Westerners had not yet fathomed the devastating consequences of the death of God. He wanted them to understand that if they gave up belief in God, they must also give up biblical ideas of morality and meaning.

Summarize the main thoughts of Nietzsche. How would you respond to him?
Nietzsche _____
_____
_____
My Response _____
_____
_____

This is exactly what the twentieth century has done. If we are not created by God—and therefore not bound by His laws—if we are simply the most advanced of the primates, why should we not do whatever we choose?

What makes this view possible is a radical dualism between body and soul, a dualism that can also be traced back to Descartes, who reduced the body to little more than a machine operated by the mind. It follows that the body is not really "me," but something separate from my real self—an instrument to be used, like a car or a computer, for whatever purposes I choose. Therefore, what I do with my body, whether I use it for physical pleasure or even discard it if it becomes inconvenient, has no moral significance.

Give an example of how the actions of some college students illustrate the above paragraph. _____
_____
_____

Carry this view to its logical conclusion, and disposing of a physical life is of no greater moral consequence than discarding an old set of ill-fitting clothes. Sexual acts between unmarried people or partners of the same sex or even complete strangers have no moral significance. Since the body is reduced to the status of a mere instrument of the conscious aspect of the self, it can be used for any form of pleasure and mutual gratification as long as there is no coercion.

The same logic is what caused the Supreme Court to decide in *Roe v. Wade* (1973) that a human fetus is not a person and can therefore legitimately be destroyed.[4] *Roe v. Wade* was the leading edge of a powerful social movement, fueled by sexual politics, to free the individual from the yoke of allegedly repressive moral restraints. "Choice" over what to do with one's body became the defining value of the 1970s and 1980s—all the while ignoring the fact that choice in itself cannot possibly be a value and that value depends on what is chosen.

The baby in the womb, having been reduced to the status of a nonperson, is then demonized in pro-choice literature as a hostile aggressor against the mother, and abortion is dressed up as self-defense. Clearly, anyone who threatens our cherished right to do whatever we please with our bodies must be stopped, by whatever means necessary. Arguing that the fetus is a violent and dangerous intruder, and justifying the use of deadly force to repel it, is the functional equivalent of Susan Smith justifying the drowning of her children with the defense that she wanted the freedom to be with her lover.

And yet many well-meaning students, including Christians, have bought into the "choice" argument. They don't see that abortion, infanticide, euthanasia, and genocide are all part of the same package. The logic that supports abortion as a "useful social policy" to prevent the birth of "defectives," or to reduce welfare and crime, applies with equal force at all stages of life. If

the body is merely an instrument of the self, if it has no inherent dignity, then we are free to dispose of it at will—or others are free to dispose of it for us.

How does the "choice" argument contradict what Christians believe? _____

_____

_____

But once this principle of autonomy and choice is established, there is no way to maintain any higher value for life. A few years ago, a former inmate whom I had discipled, and who had then gone on to become a gifted young pastor, took his own life. I was shattered when I received the news. In addition to grief, I blamed myself. I should have seen it coming, should have done something.

A friend, seeing my distress, sought to comfort me. "Don't blame yourself, Chuck," she said, gently gripping my arm, "and don't judge. It was, after all, *his* life." *His life. His choice*! The well-intentioned remark drove me deeper into despair, because this middle-aged woman reflected the beliefs of a majority of Americans.

Today, most Americans agree that it is morally acceptable to withdraw life support when the technology is merely sustaining life artificially. They also agree that it is morally acceptable to refuse extreme intervention or heroic measures to resuscitate a patient who is beyond recovery. But how quickly such distinctions can become blurred. If we have a right to refuse heroic measures and treatment, do we also have a right to ask someone to help us hasten the inevitable result?

In the end, these issues all hinge on the way a culture views human life. If human life bears the stamp of the divine Maker, it is infinitely precious. But if human life is simply a product of biology or nature, a utilitarian unit, then utilitarian values become the dominant determinant. Get the dying, the infirm, the disabled, the nonpro-

Carry this view to its logical conclusion, and disposing of a physical life is of no greater moral consequence than discarding an old set of ill-fitting clothes. Sexual acts between unmarried people or partners of the same sex or even complete strangers have no moral significance.

In the end, these issues all hinge on the way a culture views human life. If human life bears the stamp of the divine Maker, it is infinitely precious. But if human life is simply a product of biology or nature, a utilitarian unit, then utilitarian values become the dominant determinant.

ductive, out of the way of the living.

Answer the following questions. Give your reason for each of your answers.

1. A baby in a womb should not be considered a child. ❏ True ❏ False
   Because: _____
   _____
   _____

2. People have a right to choose for or against an abortion. ❏ True ❏ False
   Because: _____
   _____
   _____

3. Euthanasia is never an option.
   ❏ True ❏ False
   Because: _____
   _____
   _____

4. Christians should be involved in sanctity of life issues. ❏ True ❏ False
   Because: _____
   _____
   _____

5. All life is precious. ❏ True ❏ False
   Because: _____
   _____
   _____

Can you think of any Scriptures to support your responses? If so, go back and add the Scripture references in your reasons.

(For brochures and books on the topic of sanctity of human life, contact The Ethics and Religious Liberty Commission of the Southern Baptist Convention, 901 Commerce, Suite 550, Nashville, Tennessee 37203; 615/244-2495; www.erlc.com.)

Something within us stirs ceaselessly in search of meaning and purpose and connection. Christians know this something as the soul, or the *imago Dei*–the image of God within us. Because of the doctrine of creation, we know life has worth. We know it is rooted in something beyond the test tube or colliding atoms, even as every voice around us says otherwise.

Turn to Jeremiah 1 and answer the following questions.

1. What did the Lord say to Jeremiah? _____
   _____
   _____

2. What was Jeremiah's response? _____
   _____

3. What was God's response to Jeremiah's excuse? _____
   _____
   _____

4. What did God say to Jeremiah "the second time"? _____
   _____
   _____

✅ Points to Remember
List two key points of today's session.

1. _____
   _____

2. _____
   _____

❓ Questions to Ask
What questions do I have concerning what I've read today? _____
_____
_____
_____

👥 Actions to Take
Based on what I've read, what specific action(s) should I take? _____
_____
_____
_____

✳️ Prayers to Pray
Today, God, you taught me _____
_____
_____
_____

Help me, Lord, to _____
_____
_____
_____

Something More Important

"Your hands made me and formed me; give me under-standing to learn your commands" (Psalm 119:73).

The first question we must ask of both the Christian and the naturalistic worldviews is, "Which worldview provides the strongest basis for human dignity?"

Real Dignity
Scripture tells us that "God created man in his own image, . . . male and female he created them" (Gen. 1:27). This is a breathtaking assertion. Humans actually reflect the character of the ultimate Source of the universe. How could anyone even theoretically conceive of any more secure basis for human dignity?

The Christian worldview tells us humans have an eternal destiny, which likewise bolsters human dignity. Throughout history, most cultures have had a low view of the individual, subordinating the individual to the interests of the tribe or state. And if Christianity were not true, this would be quite reasonable. "If individuals live only seventy years," said C. S. Lewis, "then a state, or a nation, or a civilization, which may last for a thousand years, is more important than an individual. But if Christianity is true, then the individual is not only more important but incomparably more important, for he is everlasting and the life of a state or a civilization, compared with his, is only a moment."[5] This explains why Christianity has always provided not only a vigorous defense of human rights but also the sturdiest bulwark against tyranny.

And because we all stand on equal ground before God, Christianity gives a sound basis for social and political equality. What biblical support can you give for this statement?

_____

_____

_____

That's why it was the Christian conscience that was first awakened to the horrors of slavery and that launched campaigns to end it on both sides of the Atlantic. That's why the Civil Rights movement of the 1960s was led by Christians like Dr. Martin Luther King, Jr., who constantly drew on biblical mandates and appealed to the higher law of God to challenge the unjust laws of his day. That's why many of the great heroes and martyrs in the struggle against Communist tyranny in Europe were Christians like Alexandr Solzhenitsyn, Laszlo Tokes, and Jerzy Popieluszko. Since the Enlightenment, secular thinkers in the West have sought to ground human rights in human nature alone, apart from biblical revelation. Rhetoric about the "rights of man" fueled even the French Revolution. Yet without a foundation in the Christian teaching of creation, there is no way to say what human nature is. Who defines it? Who says how it ought to be treated? As a result, life is valued only as much as those in power choose to value it. Small wonder that the French Revolution, with its slogan "Neither God nor master," quickly led to tyranny and the guillotine.

It is only logical, then, to place the goal of population control over the dignity of human life and to resort to any means avail-

Yet without a foundation in the Christian teaching of creation, there is no way to say what human nature is. Who defines it? Who says how it ought to be treated? As a result, life is valued only as much as those in power choose to value it.

> *It's a staggering thought that we can know and glorify and enjoy the sovereign creator God, fulfilling His purpose through our lives. This all-consuming purpose overcomes all obstacles so that life in any circumstances has meaning and direction.*

able to reduce the human population in order to preserve Mother Nature from being depleted and despoiled. From this perspective, humans are often seen as aggressors against a pristine nature. What is the Christian's conviction on how we respond to our world? Christians believe we are responsible to protect God's creation, to be good stewards, and to exercise dominion. But naturalists go far beyond responsible environmentalism and exercising dominion.

It's hard to imagine anything more terrifying than living in a culture where human life itself is no more than a relative value. The principle we see at work here is that any culture that kills God inevitably ends up worshiping some other deity—and will gladly sacrifice even life itself, which it has reduced to a relative value, in the service of this new deity.

Take a quick look at today's newspaper. Can you identify some examples of how people are worshiping some other deity? List four examples you find below.

1. _____
2. _____
3. _____
4. _____

Real Meaning and Purpose

A second question we must ask of both the Christian and the naturalistic worldviews is, "Which worldview gives human beings a sense of meaning and purpose?"

One of the arguments often used for abortion is that children should not be brought into the world if they are destined to live in poverty or abusive situations. One of the arguments used for euthanasia is that the gravely ill have no purpose for living. These views have become common because the purpose of life has been reduced to something woefully shallow, a simplistic sense of happiness such as emotional fulfillment, career success, or wealth. Many modern Americans have lost their sense of a higher destiny.

What has been the chief end of your life as of today? Check the answers which apply to you.
- ❑ **to keep my head above the water**
- ❑ **to get the best education I can**
- ❑ **to stay out of trouble**
- ❑ **to maintain a 4.0 average**
- ❑ **to not get caught**
- ❑ **to find my mate for life**
- ❑ **to earn a masters or doctorate**
- ❑ **to fit in a fraternity or sorority**
- ❑ **to prepare myself for the real world**
- ❑ **to finish this paper**
- ❑ **to pass this course**
- ❑ **to not sleep in during class**
- ❑ **to make as much money as I can**
- ❑ **to build a portfolio**
- ❑ **to take over the family business**
- ❑ **to grow as a Christian**
- ❑ **to develop healthy parenting skills**
- ❑ **to be my own boss**
- ❑ **to have as many dates as possible**
- ❑ **(other)_____**

Now, read back over this list. Circle the statements which help you to glorify God.

The fact is, men and women cannot live without purpose; our nature is made for it. In the words of the *Westminster Shorter Catechism*:

"What is the chief end of man?" "To glorify God and enjoy Him forever."

It's a staggering thought that we can know and glorify and enjoy the sovereign creator God, fulfilling His purpose through our lives. This all-consuming purpose overcomes all obstacles so that life in any circumstances has meaning and direction.

Pleasure, freedom, happiness, prosperity—none of these is ultimately fulfilling because none can answer that ultimate question of purpose. What is the value and purpose of human life? Write your answer below.

_____
_____
_____

Knowing that we are fulfilling God's purpose is the only thing that really gives rest to the restless human heart. (Take a moment now to ask the Lord for His direction and wisdom to know and fulfill His purpose.)

Real Assurance of Destiny

A third question we must ask of both the Christian and the naturalistic worldviews is, "Which worldview can provide humans a sense of assurance about their ultimate destiny?"

Every view of human life is shaped by two great assumptions: our origin and our destiny, where we came from and where we are going. Is this life all there is? Is death the end of all our deepest aspirations and longings?

The existentialists argued that if there is nothing beyond the grave, then death makes a mockery of everything we have lived for; it reduces human projects and dreams to a temporary diversion, with no ultimate significance. In this, the existentialists were right. But if, on the contrary, our souls survive beyond the grave, as the Bible teaches, then this life is invested with profound meaning, for everything we do here has a significance for all eternity. The life of each person, whether in the womb or out, whether healthy or infirm, takes on an enormous dignity.

This is why death has always been surrounded by rituals and religious rites, for it is death that reminds us of our own mortality and forces us to ask disturbing questions about the meaning of our own life. I was forced to do this at the death of Richard Nixon. However, at the funeral, as I heard and watched Dr. Billy Graham, with millions more watching on television, he preached one of the greatest and most timely messages that I have ever heard him preach. At the funeral, he preached about Christian hope, one that no other world belief system offers.

For the secularist, death is like stepping off a cliff into a black abyss of nothingness. The Muslim faces a fearsome judgment, and for many Eastern religions, the prospect is equally grim: After death, the law of karma decrees, people must pay the penalty for what they have done in this life, being reincarnated according to their past deeds. But for the Christian, ". . . to die is gain" (read Philippians 1:21).

This is why Dietrich Bonhoeffer, a young Lutheran pastor condemned to die by Hitler, could cheerfully minister in prison to inmate and warden alike. This is why he could stop at the foot of his gallows to pray, almost in defiance of his captors, before confidently ascending the steps to be hanged. Like so many martyrs before and after him, Bonhoeffer died peacefully, infused with the confidence that comes only with the assurance of eternity.

You have been asked to write your own epitaph on your grave marker. What do you write about yourself?_____
_____
_____
_____

Real Motive for Service

A fourth question we must ask of both the Christian and the naturalistic worldviews is, "Which view of life provides the most certain motive for service and care of others?"

This is a crucial question, for any society in which citizens care only for themselves cannot long endure. Such a group cannot even be called a society. Rather, it is a collection of self-centered individuals, destined to implode when their selfish pressures reach a certain point, which is exactly what we are moving toward in our own self-absorbed culture.

Scripture commands believers to love our neighbors as ourselves, to care for widows and orphans (read James 1:27), to be a good Samaritan (read Luke 16:25), to feed the hungry, clothe the naked, visit the sick and imprisoned (read Matt. 25:36).

For the secularist, death is like stepping off a cliff into a black abyss of nothingness. The Muslim faces a fearsome judgment, and for many Eastern religions, the prospect is equally grim: After death, the law of karma decrees, people must pay the penalty for what they have done in this life, being reincarnated according to their past deeds. But for the Christian, ". . . to die is gain" (Read Philippians 1:21).

> *The Christian understands that our real hope is in the spiritual realm, so that some things are more important than biological life. Obedience to God is one of those things.*

But where does this compassion, this compulsion to care for others, come from? How do we get it? Write your answer in the space provided:_____

_____

_____

The answer is that if we know we are created by God, then we should live in a state of continuous gratitude to God. Gratitude, according to G. K. Chesterton, is the "mother of all virtues." Gratitude for every breath we breathe, every moment we have to enjoy the wonders of His creation and all that is ours—family, work, recreation. Gratitude that the Son of God took away our sins and paid our debt on the cross. Compelled by this gratitude, we desire to love Him and live as He commands. "This is love for God: to obey his commands" (1 John 5:3).

People often ask me why I've continued to work with prisoners for more than twenty-five years, to go back to prison, to frequent places rampant with disease, violence, and massive depression. My answer is simple: Out of gratitude for what Christ did for me, I can do nothing less.

Obedience to Christ's commands changes our habits and disposition. That's why, through the centuries, so many of the great humanitarian causes have been led by Christians, from abolishing the slave trade to establishing hospitals and schools. At one point in the early nineteenth century in America, there were more than eleven hundred Christian societies working for social justice. Today, two of the world's largest private organizations caring for the hungry are Christian agencies: Catholic Relief Services and World Vision. And the Salvation Army alone does more for the homeless and destitute in most areas than all secular agencies combined.

To be sure, well-meaning secularists can show compassion, give generously to charities, and offer help to the downtrodden and the needy. As creatures made in the image of God, all human beings practice some of these virtues. But the critical question is, "What motivates them?"

What do you feel motivates them? _____

_____

_____

As sociobiologists have so persuasively argued, if humans are a product of natural selection, then even the most caring acts are performed, ultimately, because they advance our own genetic interests. Kindness is a disguised form of selfishness. What this means is that even the most conscientious secularists have no rational basis for being compassionate, which means they act on solely subjective motives—which could change at any given moment.

Of course, Christians often do not follow their own convictions. But when believers fail to show compassion, they are acting contrary to their own beliefs. By contrast, when secularists do good, it is despite the internal logic of their worldview.

The high view of human life offered by Christianity is not a veneration of mere biological life. The Christian understands that our real hope is in the spiritual realm, so that some things are more important than biological life. Obedience to God is one of those things. Like a scarlet thread, such obedience winds its way from the lion's den to the cross to Bonhoeffer's gallows to Chinese house churches to services held underneath trees in the barren regions of southern Sudan. **Justice and truth are values far dearer than biological life.**

For centuries, princes, emperors, dictators, kings, and presidents have sent their subjects and citizens out to die for them. But only once in human history has a king died for his subjects. And while those princes and emperors and dictators and kings and presidents have come and gone, the one King who died for his subjects still reigns. And it is in service to Him that we find the noblest view of life and human dignity and liberty.

The naturalistic view of life pervades every area of Western culture, but nowhere with greater effect than among young adults. At every turn, you are bombarded with hedonistic, self-gratifying messages. Day in and day out, you are surrounded with the message that life is all about entertainment and pleasures and satisfying every hormonal urge. Yet deep within each of us is a truth that cannot be suppressed, even under such a relentless assault. It is in our very nature, the way we are created, no matter how hard we may try to suppress it.

Review the four questions proposed on page 43 and give a brief response to each.

1. _____
   _____
   _____
2. _____
   _____
   _____
3. _____
   _____
   _____
4. _____
   _____

Augustine, however, offered an answer that is as true today as it was sixteen hundred years ago: "You made us for yourself, and our hearts find no peace until they rest in you."[6] Only when we find God can we halt this restless search because the very essence of our nature is the *imago Dei*—the image of God—implanted in us by the Creator.

Go to the Old Testament, Psalm 119:73-80, and answer the following questions.

1. **What does the psalmist acknowledge about God?** _____
   _____
   _____
2. **What does the psalmist desire?** _____
   _____
3. **What does the psalmist delight in?**

4. **What are some of the things that the psalmist asks for and why?** _____
   _____
   _____

Points to Remember
List two key points of today's session.
1. _____
   _____
2. _____
   _____

Questions to Ask
What questions do I have concerning what I've read today? _____
_____
_____

Actions to Take
Based on what I've read, what specific action(s) should I take? _____
_____
_____

Prayers to Pray
Today, God, you taught me _____
_____
_____
_____

Help me, Lord, to _____
_____
_____
_____
_____
_____

[1] (http://www.panspermia.org/whatis2.htm).
[2] Douglas Futuyma, *Evolutionary Biology* (Sunderland, Mass.: Sinauer, 1986), 3.
[3] Friedrich Nietzsche, *The Gay Science*, trans. Walter Kaufmann (New York: Random, 1974), 125.
[4] *Roe v. Wade*, 410 US 113 (1973).
[5] C.S. Lewis, *Mere Christianity* (New York: Touchstone, 1996), 73.
[6] Saint Augustine, *Confession*, book 1, paragraph 1, trans. R.S. Pine-Coffin (New York: Penguin, 1961), 21.

Why All This Mess?

If the universe came from a wise and loving creator, why is there war and suffering, disease and death? In this session, you will focus on the Christian and utopian views of what has gone wrong with the world and how we can fix it.

DAY ONE
Explain the Human Dilemma

"Therefore, just as sin entered the world through one man, and death through sin, and in this way death came to all men, because all sinned" (Romans 5:12).

The first and fundamental element of any worldview is how it answers the question of origins—where the universe came from and how human life started. That leads to the second element, which is, how do we explain the human dilemma? Why is there war and suffering, disease and death? These questions are particularly pressing for the Christian worldview. If you believe that the universe came from the hand of a wise and good Creator, how do you explain the presence of evil?

No question poses a more formidable stumbling block to the Christian faith than this, and no question is more difficult for Christians to answer.

Yet the biblical worldview does have an answer, and it accounts for universal human experience better than any other belief system. Scripture teaches that God created the universe and created us in His image, created us to be holy, to live by His commands. Yet God loved us so much that He imparted to us the unique dignity of being free moral agents—creatures with the ability to make choices, to choose either good or evil. To provide an arena in which to exercise that freedom, God placed one moral restriction on our first ancestors: He forbade them to eat of the tree of the knowledge of good and evil. The original humans, Adam and Eve, exercised their free choice and chose to do what God had commanded them not to do, thus rejecting His way of life and goodness, opening the world to death and evil. The theological term for this catastrophe is "the Fall."

Check all Scripture references which support the above paragraph:
- ❏ Psalm 101:5,7   ❏ I Kings 11:6
- ❏ Genesis 3:22   ❏ John 3:2-5   ❏ John 8:34
- ❏ I John 1:8   ❏ I Corinthians 15:22

In short, the Bible places responsibility for sin, which opened the floodgates to evil, squarely on the human race—starting with Adam and Eve, but continuing on in our own moral choices. In that original choice to disobey God, human nature became morally distorted and bent so that from then on humanity has had a natural inclination to do wrong. This is what theologians call "original sin," and it haunts humanity to this day. And since humans were granted dominion over nature, the Fall also had cosmic consequences as nature began to bring forth "thorns and thistles," becoming a source of toil, hardship, and suffering.

What is meant by "original sin"? _____
_____
_____
_____

The problem with your answer is not that it isn't clear, but that it is unpalatable to many people because it implicates each one of us in the twisted and broken state of creation. Yet just as sin entered the world through one man, eventually implicating

Yet just as sin entered the world through one man, eventually implicating all humanity, so redemption has come to all through one man (Rom. 5:12-21).

Most influential thinkers have dismissed the idea of sin as repressive and unenlightened. They have proposed instead a utopian view that asserts that humans are intrinsically good, that under the right social conditions, their good nature will emerge.

all humanity, so redemption has come to all through one man (Rom. 5:12-21). Righteousness is available to all through belief in Christ's atoning sacrifice.

These are complex concepts, requiring fuller explanations as we go along. The Christian view of sin can seem harsh, even degrading, to human dignity. That's why in modern times, most influential thinkers have dismissed the idea of sin as repressive and unenlightened. They have proposed instead a utopian view that asserts that humans are intrinsically good, that under the right social conditions, their good nature will emerge. This utopian view has roots in the Enlightenment, when Western intellectuals rejected the biblical teaching of creation and replaced it with the theory that nature is our creator—that the human race had arisen out of the primordial slime and lifted itself to the apex of evolution. Under the utopian view college students would no longer live under the shadow of guilt and moral judgment; no longer would they be oppressed and hemmed in by moral rules imposed by an arbitrary and tyrannical deity. The biblical doctrine of sin was cast aside, a holdover from what Enlightenment philosophers disdainfully called the Dark Ages, from which their own age had so triumphantly emerged.

What is meant by the "utopian view"? _____
_____
_____
_____
_____

But if the problem is not sin, then what is the source of disorder and suffering? Enlightenment thinkers concluded that these must be the product of the environment: ignorance, poverty, or other undesirable social conditions. Hence, all it takes to create an ideal society is a better environment: improved education, enhanced economic conditions, and reengineered social structures. Given the right conditions,

human perfectibility has no limits. Thus was born the modern utopian impulse.

Yet which of these worldviews, the biblical one or the modern utopian one, meets the test of reality? Which fits the world and human nature as we actually experience it?

One can hardly say that the biblical view of sin is unrealistic, with its frank acknowledgment of the human disposition to make wrong moral choices and inflict harm and suffering on others. Not when we view the long sweep of history.

By contrast, the "enlightened" worldview has proven to be utterly irrational and unlivable. The denial of our sinful nature, and the utopian myth it breeds, leads not to beneficial social experiments but to tyranny. The confidence that college students are perfectible provides a justification for trying to make them perfect . . . no matter what it takes. And with God out of the picture, those in power are not accountable to any higher authority. They can use any means necessary, no matter how brutal or coercive, to remold students to fit their notion of the perfect society.

The triumph of the Enlightenment worldview, with its fundamental change in presuppositions about human nature was, in many ways, the defining event of the twentieth century, which explains why the history of this era is so tragically written in blood. As William Buckley trenchantly observes: Utopianism "inevitably brings on the death of liberty."[1]

Share two reasons you feel a denial of our sinful nature would "lead to tyranny."
1. _____
_____
2. _____
_____

The denial of sin and responsibility is couched in therapeutic terms, such as the need to "understand" even the worst crimes as a result of a dysfunctional childhood or other circumstances.

Against the utopian worldview, we will pose the Christian worldview, which we submit is demonstrably the only philosophy that fits universal human experience.

Good and Evil, Right and Wrong

What did become of sin? Good question. To solve the mystery, we must travel back to the mid-eighteenth century and to the influential writings of a young Swiss-born philosopher named Jean-Jacques Rousseau. Rousseau burst upon the European intellectual scene, winning instant notoriety with an essay arguing a surprising thesis: that the progress of civilization had been harmful for human beings, not beneficial. In its natural state, human nature is good, he contended; people become evil only when they are corrupted by society.

From the time of Aristotle, most philosophers had taught that humans are naturally social and that they fulfill their true nature by participating in the civilizing institutions of family, church, state, and society. But Rousseau insisted that human nature was at its best prior to and apart from social institutions; that people are naturally loving, virtuous, and selfless; and that it is society, with its artificial rules and conventions, that makes them envious, hypocritical, and competitive.

Identify two elements of Rousseau's thesis.

1. _____
   _____

2. _____
   _____

The time in which Rousseau lived was noted as an artificial society. Men pranced about in long, curly, powdered wigs. He denounced it false to the core, and he retreated to small country houses where he could be close to nature. He delighted shocking people by wearing bizarre flowing robes and caftans. He refused to practice accepted manners or social formalities.

Rousseau's odd dress and crude manners were a deliberate expression of his philosophy: If human nature is essentially good, if evil and corruption are created by a false and hypocritical society, then throw off the restraints of civilization and explore your natural, spontaneous self–the true self that underlies social forms. Free it from stultifying pressures to conform.

Think about a few groups on your campus. How does their style of dress and manner communicate their beliefs or message? Call them Group 1 and Group 2.

Group 1: _____
_____
_____
_____
_____
_____

Group 2: _____
_____
_____
_____
_____
_____

These same ideas appear in Rousseau's formal writing on philosophy. He rejected anything that limits the freedom of the inner self, which he saw as naturally good—or, at least, unformed and undefined and capable of being made good. His most influential work, *The Social Contract and Discourses*, opens with the famous line, "Man is born free, and everywhere he is in chains."[2] Since individuals start out unformed, they must be free to create themselves by their own choices, free to discover their own identity, free to follow their own road. The goal of the individual is to be set free from the chains of institutions, rules, customs, and traditions.

Moreover, since human nature is essentially undefined, according to Rousseau, there are no moral principles limiting the state's ambitions. In the Christian world-

Jean-Jacques Rousseau (1712-1778)

Born in Geneva, Rousseau's mother died at his birth, and his father eventually deserted him.

Rousseau tried two apprenticeships but ran away to escape the discipline. After attending school, he served in households, and was charged with theft in one. After more wandering, he spent eight years enjoying nature and studying.

Rousseau's life was marked with both dismal failures and great acclamation.

view, we treat a thing according to its nature, the type of being it is, based ultimately on what God created it to be. That's why we treat a child differently from a dog. But if there is no such thing as human nature, then there is no justification for saying we should treat people one way rather than another. There is no basis for saying the state must treat its citizens justly instead of unjustly, and hence there are no moral limitations on the state's use of power.

A Peculiar Blindness

Why didn't anyone in Rousseau's legions of disciples see that absolute power is sure to corrupt?

Because utopianism creates a peculiar blindness. Believing the individual to be naturally good, Rousseau was confident that the all-powerful state would likewise be good, since the state was simply a merging of individual wills into a "General Will." Consequently, Rousseau actually believed that the General Will would always be right, always tending toward the public good—"always constant, unalterable, and pure."[3] And if some recalcitrant individuals failed to agree with the General Will? That merely proved that they had been corrupted and that they must be coerced into seeing that their true liberty lay in conforming to the General Will. As Rousseau put it, the individual must "be forced to be free."[4]

This same basic pattern can be seen in the philosophy of Karl Marx, whose vision of a perfect society has fueled one failed utopian experiment after another in nations around the globe. The fatal flaw in Marxism's utopian view of the state is once again the denial of the basic Christian teaching of the Fall. If one is to believe there is such a thing as sin, one must believe there is a God who is the basis of a transcendent and universal standard of goodness. Marx denied all of this. For him, religion and morality were nothing but ideologies used to rationalize the economic interests of one class over another. Small wonder that the totalitarian states created by Marxism acknowledged no universal moral principles, no transcendent justice, and no moral limits on their murderous brutality. The party, like the General Will, was always right.

The same denial of sin explains the roots of fascism. In 1964, *Time* magazine was a latecomer in raising the question on its front cover, "Is God Dead?" Back in the nineteenth century, German philosopher Friedrich Nietzsche had already declared the death of God and had etched out what that would mean: the death of morality. Nietzsche, one of the most powerful influences on fascism, dismissed sin as nothing but a ruse invented by a wretched band of "ascetic priest[s]," Old Testament shamans who had achieved a magical hold over men and women by playing the "ravishing music" of guilt in their souls.[5] And he de-

Contrast Rousseau's philosophy with the Christian worldview on these issues.

	ROUSSEAU'S PHILOSOPHY	CHRISTIAN WORLDVIEW
Transforming human nature		
Moral principles Public good		
True liberty		

nounced Christian morality as a morality for slaves. Kindness, forgiveness, humility, obedience, self-denial—these were the characteristics of weak, repressed slaves who had rejected the joy of life. In Nietzsche's mind, the biblical ethic was nothing less than a pathology, a life-killing prudery. He looked forward to the evolution of a race of superhumans imbued with an ethic of power—exactly what the Nazis hoped to create from the Aryan race.

Identify two or more ways the following two individuals reflect the philosophy of Rousseau.

Karl Marx-

1. _____

_____

2. _____

_____

3. _____

_____

Friedrich Nietzsche-

1. _____

_____

2. _____

_____

3. _____

_____

Ideas do not arise from the intellect alone. They reflect our whole personality, our hopes and fears, our longings and regrets. People who follow a particular course of action are inevitably subject to intellectual pressure to find a rationale for it. Theologians call this the "noetic" effect of sin, meaning that sin affects our minds, our thinking processes. The Reformers coined the phrase "total depravity," meaning that our sinful choices distort all aspects of our being, including our theoretical ideas.

Turn to Romans 5 and answer the following questions.

1. **How does a college student experience "peace with God"?** _____

_____

_____

_____

2. **For whom did Christ die?** _____

_____

_____

_____

3. **How are we "reconciled to God"?** _____

_____

_____

_____

4. **How did sin enter the world?** _____

_____

_____

_____

5. **What is the result of sin?** _____

_____

_____

_____

_____

✅ Points to Remember

List two key points of today's session.

1. _____

_____

2. _____

_____

❓ Questions to Ask

What questions do I have concerning what I've read today? _____

_____

_____

👥 Actions to Take

Based on what I've read, what specific action(s) should I take? _____

_____

_____

_____

_____

_____

Friedrich Nietzsche (1844-1900)

Nietzsche was born on October 15, 1844, in Röcken, Prussia. His father, a Lutheran minister, died when Nietzsche was four, and he was raised by his mother. He was convinced that traditional values represented a "slave morality," a morality created by weak and resentful individuals who encouraged such behavior as gentleness and kindness because the behavior served their interests. Nietzsche claimed that new values could be created to replace the old ones.

DAY TWO
Scientific Utopianism

"If we claim to be without sin, we deceive ourselves, and the truth is not in us" (1 John 1:8).

If we turn students and all humans into objects for scientific study, we implicitly assume that they are objects to be manipulated and controlled, like scientific variables. That means we have to deny things like the soul, conscience, moral reasoning, and moral responsibility.

In the eighteenth and nineteenth centuries, social thinkers fervently believed that science would not only explain the physical world but also show us how to order our lives together harmoniously. To that end, they searched for some principle that would explain society in the same way Newton's law of gravity explained motion. They sought an experimental physics of the soul that would enable them to craft a science of government and politics to conquer the age-old plagues of ignorance and oppression, poverty and war.

Of course, nowhere has this vision of scientific utopianism become a reality, and the reason it continually fails is lodged in the logic of the scientific method itself. If we turn students and all humans into objects for scientific study, we implicitly assume that they are objects to be manipulated and controlled, like scientific variables. That means we have to deny things like the soul, conscience, moral reasoning, and moral responsibility. And when we apply these assumptions to real social problems, we inevitably dehumanize and demoralize people, placing them at the mercy of social scientists in the employ of the technocratic state. In short, by denying moral responsibility, we end up not with utopia but with another form of despotism.

This line of logic can be seen clearly in the field of psychology. Sigmund Freud did more than anyone else to debunk the very notion of moral responsibility. Freud reduced humans to complex animals, rejecting explanations of behavior couched in "old-fashioned" theological terms—like sin, soul, and conscience—and substituting scientific terms borrowed from biology, such as instincts and drives. In Freud's theory, people are not so much rational agents as pawns in the grip of unconscious forces they do not understand and cannot control.

Psychologists who followed Freud carried this process of reduction even further by seeing humans not as animals but as machines. The earliest book on experimental psychology was titled *Elements of Psychophysics*, as if psychology were a branch of physics. Its author, Gustav Fechner, argued that humans are complicated stimulus-response mechanisms, shaped by the forces of their environment.[6]

How did Freud try to disprove the notion of moral responsibility? _____

_____

_____

After Fechner came Ivan Pavlov, whose name we all know because of his experiments conditioning dogs to salivate at the ringing of a bell. Pavlov, an evolutionist and materialist, adamantly rejected any notion of soul, spirit, or consciousness. All mental life, he declared (whether in his salivating dogs or in human beings), could be explained in entirely mechanical terms of stimulus and response.[7]

In the 1960s, B. F. Skinner's *Walden Two* introduced millions of college students to behaviorism, a school of psychology that flatly denies the reality of consciousness or mental states. Because these things cannot be observed, Skinner argued, they cannot be described scientifically; therefore, they are not real. Only observable, external behavior is real.[8]

By denying the reality of the mind, Skinner and the behaviorists believed they were "purifying" psychology of all philosophical prejudices and rendering it purely scientific and objective. In reality, of course, they were simply injecting their own philosophical prejudices. They were also creating a new brand of scientific utopianism, which said that the flaws in human nature are a result not of moral corruption but of learned responses—responses that can be unlearned so that people can then be reprogrammed to be happy and adjusted, living in harmony in a utopian society.

Briefly describe what Pavlov and Skinner attempted to prove.

Pavlov: _____

_____

_____

Skinner: _____

_____

_____

_____

- One the of results of this utopian thinking was a shift in education. Education became a means of conditioning, with the person being treated as essentially passive (rather than as an active moral agent).

What is the danger of a person being treated as a "passive learner" rather than an "active moral agent"? _____

_____

_____

_____

- The same ideas were applied to law. The law was redefined as a tool for identifying and manipulating the right factors to create social harmony and progress.
- And the same scientific utopianism explains the rise of the welfare state. The idea that both law and government policy should be transformed into social engineering took root in the New Deal of the 1930s and blossomed in the Great Society programs of the 1960s.

The welfare state has backfired, creating both a near-permanent underclass of dependency and a host of attendant social pathologies, from broken families and little morality to drug abuse and crime. What went wrong?

Again we see the supreme irony. When we deny the Christian worldview and reject its teachings on sin and moral responsibility in favor of a more "enlightened" and "scientific" view of human nature, we actually end up stripping people of their dignity and treating them as less than human.

By ignoring the moral dimension, by reducing social disorders to technical problems to be addressed with scientific solutions, we have created moral chaos.

Give one way you feel scientific utopianism has backfired. _____

_____

_____

Scientific utopianism expands government control while gradually sapping citi-

Sigmund Freud (1856-1939)

Born in Freiberg, Moravia (today Czech Republic) Sigmund Freud was an Austrian neurologist and psychologist. He founded psychoanalysis. He divided the mind into the id, ego, and superego.

Freud's theory of the human mind has come to dominate modern thought. His theories and terminology have shaped not just the field of psychology. They have become the standard way modern people understand themselves.

By ignoring the moral dimension, by reducing social disorders to technical problems to be addressed with scientific solutions, we have created moral chaos.

In denying sin and evil, we actually unleash its worst powers.

zens of moral responsibility, economic initiative, and personal prudence.

In your opinion, why has America's staggering crime rate from the 1960s through the 1980s demonstrated that both liberal and conservative approaches to criminal justice have failed?

❏ _____
❏ _____
❏ _____
❏ _____

Why? Because neither recognizes the dignity of the soul and its ability to make morally significant choices. Neither respects human beings as genuine moral agents, capable of both real good and real evil. And neither addresses the need for moral responsibility and repentance.

List two reasons why criminal justice has failed.

1. _____
2. _____

Share two ways you have noticed these "failures" around your own campus.

1. _____
_____
2. _____
_____

Denial of sin may appear to be a benign and comforting doctrine, but in the end, it is demeaning and destructive, for it also denies the significance of our choices and actions. In doing this, it reduces us to pawns in the grip of larger forces: either unconscious forces in the human psyche or economic and social forces in the environment.

What will result when we do not address our sin problem? _____
_____
_____
_____

What about you? How are you addressing the issue of sin and forgiveness in your own life?

Utopianism depends on a kind of willful blindness to the reality of human sin and moral responsibility. But in denying the reality of sin, we lose the capacity to deal with it, and thus, in the end, we actually compound its effects. Therein lies the greatest paradox of all attempts to deny the Fall: In denying sin and evil, we actually unleash its worst powers.

Turn to 1 John 1 and answer the following questions.

1. What is the main message of this chapter?
_____
_____

2. Under what condition does a person "lie"?
_____
_____

3. When do we have "fellowship with one another"?
_____

4. Under what condition do we "deceive ourselves"? _____
_____

5. What takes place when we "confess our sins"? _____
_____
_____

✅ Points to Remember
List two key points of today's session.
1. _____
_____
2. _____
_____

❓ Questions to Ask
What questions do I have concerning what I've read today? _____
_____

_____
_____
_____

✴ Prayers to Pray

Today, God, you taught me _____
_____
_____
_____
_____

✿ Actions to Take

Based on what I've read, what specific action(s) should I take? _____
_____
_____
_____

Help me, Lord, to _____
_____
_____
_____

DAY THREE
The Face of Evil

"For we are God's workmanship, created in Christ Jesus to do good works, which God prepared in advance for us to do" (Ephesians 2:10).

What does the face of evil look like?

List three people in history who could be the answers to this question. Give your reason for listing each person.

1. _____ Because: _____
_____

2. _____ Because: _____
_____

3. _____ Because: _____
_____

A few years ago when I visited a South Carolina women's prison, I learned that Susan Smith had signed up to hear me speak. Smith is the woman who deliberately allowed her car to slide into a lake with her two small sons still strapped in their car seats. Her reason? She wanted to be free of children when she married the man she was dating.

As I prepared to speak that day, I scanned the audience, wondering what this unnatural mother would look like. I imagined some kind of female Dorian Gray, her face marked by the soul-struggle she had waged with evil. Recalling photos from the newspaper, I searched for her face, but I couldn't pick her out.

After the meeting, I asked the local Prison Fellowship director whether Smith had even attended. "Oh, sure." he replied. "She was in the front row, staring at you the whole time."

The face of evil is frighteningly ordinary.

In Austin, Texas, Charles Whitman climbs to the top of a tower with a high powered gun. He begins to shoot anyone he sees. When the episode was over, 31 students were wounded and 16 people were dead .

On the campus of a prestigious school in Nashville, TN, a student was stabbed to death by another student. The reason: the other student needed money and took another persons life to get it.

On many campuses the issue of "razing" has been banned by the administration because of the harm it inflicts on fellow students. In some cases, fraternities have been placed on probation and even banned from the campus for promoting this form of initiation.

In New Jersey, Brian Peterson takes his girlfriend, Amy Grossberg, across the state line to a Delaware hotel room, where she gives birth. They kill the newborn and dump him in the trash. [9]

To the side of each of these five examples, write a word describing your emotion of how you now feel about that situation.

1. Killers with high grades. Killers who, depressed, go out to get someone, anyone.

2. Killers in the classroom. Killers who order pizza and go to "Greek" meetings.

3. What does the face of evil look like? It looks like the student next door. It looks like us.

4. How can we look at this carnage, this unspeakable evil lurking behind the wholesome smile of a college student, and still cling to the myth that humans are basically good?

5. Media coverage of these heinous crimes offered all the conventional answers.

The problem is poverty. (But most of these killers were middle class.) The problem is race—for there is a hushed racism in much of our perception of crime. (But all these perpetrators were white.) The problem is a dysfunctional childhood—the therapeutic catch-phrase these days for all ab-

normal behavior. (But millions of students come from harsh circumstances and never commit a crime.)

The only explanation not offered is the one that modern commentators cannot bring themselves to say: the dreaded "*s* word". . . sin. It is sin that unleashes the capacity for raw evil. It is sin that blinds us to anything beyond our own selfish desire.

Sin is choosing what we know is wrong. Rewrite this sentence in your own words:
_____
_____

How have we lost touch with such a fundamental truth? To begin to answer this, just look at the way children are raised today. Students are taught, above all else, to like themselves. Grammatical errors go uncorrected lest a red mark damage the student's self-esteem. "Guilt" is something hazardous to mental well-being, an artificial constraint from which we need to be liberated.

As a result, where do you see this type of classroom behavior heading? _____
_____
_____

Today's generation does not even understand the vocabulary of moral responsibility. Is it surprising, then, that we now have students who show no remorse when they violate the rights of others, from trivial things like stealing a sister's blouse to horrific crimes like gunning down a classmate?

Even in the home, the heart and hearth of society, a sense of duty has been replaced by a sense of entitlement, a sense that we have a right to what we want, even if it means violating standards of proper behavior. Adults who once gave firm and unequivocal moral direction—parents, teachers, even pastors—have been indoctrinated with the idea that the way to ensure healthy children is not to tell them what's right and wrong but to let them discover their own values.

As a result, where do you see this type of home behavior heading? _____

_____

Most college students have lost even the vocabulary of moral accountability. Sin and moral responsibility have become alien concepts. The utopian mind-set has become so pervasive that most college students in Western culture have no intellectual resources to identify or deal with genuine wrongdoing.

In what ways have you been affected? _____

_____

_____

The fatal flaw in the myth of human goodness is that it simply fails to correspond with what we know about the world from our own ordinary experience. And when a worldview is too small, when it denies the existence of some part of reality, that part will reassert itself in some way, demanding our attention. It's like trying to squeeze a balloon in your hands: some parts will always bulge out. Our sense of sin always finds expression in some form.

Take, for example, the enormous appetite college students have for horror fiction. What explains this fascination? Part of the answer may be that these books deal with gnawing questions about the depth of human evil. This may be one reason Stephen King's novels top the charts again and again. For in King's gruesome world, evil is threateningly real, and supernatural forces lurk everywhere, seeking whom they may devour. Normal students are drawn to these grim stories for the same reason a small child wants to hear the story of the "Three Little Pigs" over and over again, each time delighting in the way the resourceful third pig heats a pot of boiling water in his fireplace to scald the big bad wolf when he sneaks down the chimney.

What children's stories or movies can you recall which exposed you to evil characters?

_____

_____

How have these stories/movies influenced your thinking today? _____

_____

For college students, fiction can provide a similar function: a way of confronting the dark side of reality. Novelist Susan Wise Bauer says young adults living in a world of tragedy and pain "need a Grimm for grown-ups—a narrative that not only explains the presence of evil but offers a triumph over it."[10]

In our therapeutic age, we have been taught that "one form of behavior is as valid as another," that even murder and destruction must not be condemned but understood, Horror/thriller writer Dean Koontz says. "In 'enlightened' thought there is no true evil." But in our daily life, we know this isn't true. This explains why "people gravitate to fiction that says there is true evil, that there is a way to live that is good, and that there is a way to live that is bad. And that these are moral choices." People have an "inner need to see what they really know on a gut level about life reflected in the entertainment they view or the literature they read."[11]

In a world where juries excuse the inexcusable, where psychologists explain away the unimaginable, college students like you are groping for a kind of realism that you find, ironically, in fiction.

The fact is that a utopian framework has taken away the conceptual tools we need to grapple effectively with genuine evil. For when we cannot name or identify something, we lose the capacity to deal with it—and in the case of evil, ultimately we compound its deadly effects.

In any society, only two forces hold the

Sociologists are constantly searching for the root causes of crime and other dysfunctions in society. But the root cause has not changed since the temptation in the garden of Eden. It is sin.

sinful nature in check: the restraint of conscience or the restraint of the sword. The less that citizens have of the former, the more the state must employ the latter. A society that fails to keep order by an appeal to civic duty and moral responsibility must resort to coercion—either open coercion, as practiced by totalitarian states, or covert coercion, where citizens are wooed into voluntarily giving up their freedom. Given the examples cited at the beginning of today's session, it's not much of a stretch to imagine college students eventually so frightened of their own peers and other adults that they will welcome protection by ever-greater government control. That's why utopianism always leads to the loss of liberty.

In your opinion, what is the only hope for our society? _____
_____

The only alternative to increased state control is to be honest about the human condition. The only solution for the pathologies that plague our society is to expose the modern myth of human goodness and to return to biblical realism. Sociologists are constantly searching for the root causes of crime and other dysfunctions in society. But the root cause has not changed since the temptation in the garden of Eden. It is sin.

Human beings have revolted against God and His created order, throwing the entire creation out of joint. Everything is distorted by sin. Nothing is free from its effects. This is not merely a "religious" message, limited to some "private" realm of faith. It is the truth about ultimate reality, a truth we need to look at more closely. As we do, we see clearly why the biblical worldview provides the only rational basis for living in the real world.

Turn to Ephesians 2:1-10 and answer the following questions.

1. **Prior to becoming a Christian, how does a person "walk"?** _____
_____
_____

2. **What are God's actions toward us?** _____
_____
_____

3. **Rewrite verses 8 and 9 in your own words.**
_____
_____

4. **What does it mean to be God's "workmanship"?** _____
_____
_____

✅ Points to Remember
List two key points of today's session.
1. _____
_____
2. _____
_____

❓ Questions to Ask
What questions do I have concerning what I've read today? _____
_____
_____
_____

👥 Actions to Take
Based on what I've read, what specific action(s) should I take? _____
_____
_____
_____

✳ Prayers to Pray
Today, God, you taught me _____
_____
_____
_____
_____

Help me, Lord, to _____
_____
_____
_____

Understanding the Moral Dilemma

"Teach me your way, O Lord, and I will walk in your truth; give me an undivided heart, that I may fear your name" (Psalm 86:11).

God not only gave the first two human beings, Adam and Eve, a genuine moral choice, but He also set a moral limit.

Read Genesis 2:16-17.
What two choices did Adam and Eve have to make?

1. _____
   _____

2. _____
   _____

Adam and Eve were free either to believe God and obey His law or to disobey Him and suffer the consequences. This same choice confronts every person throughout history.

To disobey God is to choose death because disobedience ultimately leads to total alienation from God. To obey is to choose life. Obedience is not just a matter of following rules arbitrarily imposed by a harsh master; obedience is a means of entering into real life, a life rich in meaning and purpose.

Read Deuteronomy 30:15,19.
To disobey God is to choose _____.
To obey God is to choose _____.

Obedience is also not simply about external acts. Obedience is an internal response to God as a personal being.

What does Deuteronomy 6:5 say about our relationship with God?_____
_____
_____
_____

At the core of God's commandments is not a set of principles or a list of expectations; at the heart of God's commandments is a *relationship*. We are to love God with our
_____. What about those consequences?

God is good, and all of His original creation was good; He is not the author of evil. Evil entered the world solely through the free choice of His creatures. This is a crucial element in Christian teaching, for if God had created evil, then His own essence would contain both good and evil, and there would be no hope that good could ever triumph over evil.

The biblical teaching of the original goodness of creation solves two important philosophical problems: It explains the source of evil, and it grounds our hope of personal salvation. If we had been created with a fatal flaw, then salvation would require destroying us and starting over. But since we were created good, salvation means restoring us to what we were originally created to be. Redemption means the restoration and fulfillment of God's original purposes.

To disobey God is to choose death because disobedience ultimately leads to total alienation from God. To obey is to choose life.

List two problems solved by the biblical teaching of the original goodness of creation.

1. _____
   _____
2. _____
   _____

But if God is good and creation is good, what is the ultimate origin of evil? Again we turn to the early pages of Genesis, where we are told about the temptation of Eve by a powerful spiritual being who appeared in the form of a serpent and insinuated his destructive ideas simply by raising questions.

What question did the serpent raise in Genesis 3:1? _____

_____

What did the serpent announce in Genesis 3:4? _____

_____

How was this a blatant confrontation of truth with a lie? _____

_____

One of the main characters in the Biblical drama is a fallen angel, a once-perfect being who made a moral decision to rebel against God. This being is called "the accuser" or "Satan" or "the devil."

Draw a line from the action of Satan to the identifying Scripture reference.

Searching for souls to corrupt	**1 Peter 5:8**
Looking for someone to devour	**John 8:44**
Entered into a person's life	**John 1:7**
Is a liar	**Isaiah 14:14**

Intention is to be like God

John 13:27

A new Christian convert once asked me, "Aren't Adam and Eve just symbols for all humanity, and isn't the Fall merely a symbol of the sin that traps us all?"

What response would you give to this question? _____

_____

No, Adam and Eve are not characters in a mythical fable. These were real human beings who made real choices. As the apostle Paul declares again and again in Romans 5, Adam and Eve's fall into sin was as historical as Christ's redemption on Calvary, and the two are inextricably joined. Because the Fall was genuinely historical, the second person of the Trinity had to enter history and suffer death and resurrection to bring about redemption.

The biblical explanation of evil is not merely an intellectual exercise or a theoretical way to explain what's wrong with the rest of the world. Instead, it carries an unavoidable personal message: that each of us has sinned against a holy God.

Read Romans 3:10-12 and share what message it gives to you. _____

_____

_____

_____

When we truly understand these words, we are gripped by a profound humility, for we realize that we all come into this world with equal moral standing before God and that our condition is desperate apart from the redemption that God alone can provide.

But, the skeptic asks, what about the person who never hears the gospel? How does Romans 1:19-20 answer this question?

The apostle Paul tells us that we are all without excuse. We are accountable for what we know (and by implication not for what we don't know). And when by our own actions we rebel against what we know to be right and true, we eventually pay the consequences.

Even so, God always leaves us a way out. He is ready, willing, and able to forgive and restore us. Full redemption is God's provision for sparing us the consequences we would otherwise rightly deserve.

The consequences of sin affect the very order of the universe itself. Most people have a narrow understanding of the term sin, believing it to mean that we broke a few rules, we made a few mistakes. So we apologize and get on with our lives, right? Wrong. Sin is much more than breaking the rules. God created an intricate, interwoven cosmos, each part depending on the others, all governed by laws of order and harmony. Sin affects every part of that order and harmony—twisting, fracturing, distorting, and corrupting it.

First, sin disrupts our relationship with God. What was the first thing Adam and Eve did after they ate the forbidden fruit? They tried to hide from God. Because of sin, humans feel guilty and afraid of God.

Second, sin alienates us from each other. Adam immediately began to blame Eve for his action, and Eve blamed the serpent for tempting her.

Third, the Fall affected all of nature. Because Adam and Eve were given dominion over the rest of creation, their rebellion injected disorder into all of creation. Scripture clearly teaches that sin ruptured the physical as well as the moral order. Thus it was that God warned Eve that, as a consequence of sin, childbearing and family life would become a matter of pain and sorrow (see Gen. 3). Certainly it is in our intimate family relationships that we suffer the deepest heartbreak. God also warned Adam that when he tried to cultivate the earth to grow food, it would produce "thorns and thistles" (Gen. 3:17-19). Work, which was originally creative and fulfilling, would become a matter of drudgery and toil.

Finally, God told Adam and Eve that they would return to the dust from which they were taken. In other words, death and its preliminaries—sickness and suffering—would become part of the human experience.

Clearly, the Fall was not just an isolated act of disobedience that could be quickly mended. Every part of God's good handiwork was marred by this human mutiny.

For example, sexuality is good, created by God; but it is often distorted by lust and unfaithfulness. At the Fall, every part of creation was plunged into the chaos of sin, and every part cries out for redemption. Only the Christian worldview keeps these two truths in balance: the radical destruction caused by sin and the hope of the restoration to the original goodness of creation.

Write out these four consequences of sin.

1. Sin _____ our _____ with God.
2. Sin _____ us from _____.
3. The _____ affects all of _____.
4. _____, _____, and world _____ become part of the _____ experience.

Only the Christian worldview allows us to cope with the dilemmas we face daily, giving us a rational way to understand and order our lives. An exchange in a college ethics class illustrates this well. During a discussion on the nature of moral responsibility, one student asked, "Who are we responsible to? After all, the notion of responsibility makes no sense unless we are responsible to someone."

"We're responsible to other people," another student volunteered. "For example, if you run over a child, you're responsible to the child's parents."

"But who says?" persisted the first student. "Who will hold me accountable to those parents?"

"It's society we're responsible to," ventured a third student. "Society sets up the laws that we follow, and it holds us accountable."

"But who gives society that right?" asked the first student.

If you were a part of this class, what would you have done? (Circle your response.)
❑ I would have kept quiet.
❑ I would have whispered a comment to a friend beside me.
❑ I would have "checked out" mentally.
❑ I would have said, "_____."

The answer lurking in many minds in that classroom was that our ultimate responsibility is to God. Any other authority can be challenged. Only if there is an absolute Being, a Being of perfect goodness and justice, is there an ultimate tribunal before which we are all accountable. But in a secular university classroom, no one dared say that. So the students debated back and forth, hoping to find some basis for moral accountability that would not require them to acknowledge divine authority.

We need to press our skeptical neighbors to compare worldviews. Denying the reality of sin may appear to be enlightened and uplifting, but ultimately it is demeaning and destructive. Christianity, on the other hand, enables us to realistically address societal issues such as welfare, crime, human rights, and education. Christianity provides the basis for a welfare system that is both compassionate and morally challenging, reinforcing recipients' dignity and self respect. Christianity undergirds a criminal justice system that holds people accountable for their actions rather than reducing their stature as moral agents through the psychobabble of victimization. Christianity affords the basis for a solid theory of human rights, regarding all individuals as equally created by God and equally fallen. Christian education treats children

with the dignity of beings made in the image of God. In each of these areas, as we have seen in the preceding chapters, an objective comparison exposes the utter bankruptcy of modern utopianism and its tenet of natural goodness.

How Are You Handling Sin in Your Own Life?

Of course, the notion of sin is not just a worldview issue; it is also intensely personal. On that level, a realistic grasp of human depravity drives us to God in our search for a solution to our personal guilt. Instead of trying to bury it under layers of psychological jargon—where it never stays buried—we can face our guilt head-on, knowing that God Himself has provided a way out.

Read Psalm 86 and answer the following questions.

1. What is David asking of God in verses 1-7?

_____
_____
_____
_____

2. Why does David refer to God as "great"?

_____
_____
_____
_____

3. How can a person walk in God's truth?

_____
_____
_____
_____

✅ Points to Remember
List two key points of today's session.
1. _____
_____
2. _____
_____

? Questions to Ask
What questions do I have concerning what I've read today? _____

_____

_____

👥 Actions to Take
Based on what I've read, what specific action(s) should I take? _____

_____

_____

✳ Prayers to Pray
Today, God, you taught me _____

_____

_____

_____

_____

Help me, Lord, to _____

_____

_____

DAY FIVE
False Solutions

"I consider that our present sufferings are not worth comparing with the glory that will be revealed in us" *(Romans 8:18).*

For Albert Einstein, the greatest scientist of this century, the toughest intellectual barrier to Christian faith was not the question of whether God created the world. He saw clearly that the universe is designed and orderly, and he concluded that it must, therefore, be the result of a mind, not merely of matter bumping around endlessly in space. As he put it, the order of the universe "reveals an intelligence of such superiority" that it overshadows all human intelligence. His famous quip, "God does not play dice with the universe," though directed specifically against quantum theory, reveals his fierce commitment to a causal order unifying nature from top to bottom.

What stymied Einstein was something much tougher than the doctrine of creation: it was the problem of evil and suffering. Knowing there must be a designer, he agonized over the character of that de-

signer. How could God be good yet allow the terrible things that happen to people? And because Einstein could not reconcile the problem of evil and suffering with a good God, he turned away from the God of the Bible.

What answer could you give for the question above? _____

_____

_____

_____

Who would Einstein say was responsible for evil? God Himself, Einstein had to conclude. If an omnipotent God exists, he said, there must be a kind of divine determinism, where God winds us up and makes us act the way we do. But if God makes us do bad things as well as good things, then He is directly responsible for evil. "In giving out punishments and rewards, he would to

> *What stymied Einstein was something much tougher than the doctrine of creation: it was the problem of evil and suffering.*

Some people solve the problem of evil by denying that God exists at all.

a certain extent be passing judgment on himself," Einstein wrote. "How can this be combined with the goodness and righteousness ascribed to him?" If our actions are determined, then God Himself must be evil. [12]

Unwilling to accept the hopelessness of a belief system in which the ultimate reality is evil, Einstein concluded that the only God that exists is an impersonal cosmic mind giving the world its rational structure. Einstein meant only that he believed in the principle of order in the universe. To Einstein, then, true religion was nothing more than rapture before the rational structure of the universe.

Einstein was nothing if not logical. But a person's conclusion is only as good as his premise, and Einstein's premise that humans are essentially robots was seriously flawed. He missed the truth of Judaism (into which he was born) and of Christianity (which he also investigated) not because he was forced to by "the facts" but because he had already committed himself to a particular philosophy of human nature—a philosophy that prevented him from reconciling the problem of suffering and evil with the existence of a good God.

Many people share Einstein's predicament, finding the problem of evil and suffering a major stumbling block to Christian faith. So how can we respond? Does the Bible offer a sound answer that makes sense of suffering? Can Christianity answer the heart's demand for justice in a fallen universe?

How would you respond to these questions?
1. _____
2. _____
3. _____
4. _____

To see the problem clearly, let's state it in simple propositions. If God is both all-good and all-powerful, He will not allow evil and suffering to exist in His creation. Yet evil does exist. Therefore, either God is not all-good (that's why He tolerates evil), or He is not all-powerful (that's why He can't get rid of evil, even though He wants to). Throughout history, people have grappled with this apparent contradiction and have proposed a variety of solutions, all of which fall short of the biblical solution. Since we encounter these solutions again and again, it is important to know how to debunk them. Let's examine some false solutions.

Some people solve the problem of evil by denying that God exists at all. The atheists take the most direct strategy and throw out the first proposition. If there is no God, then evil poses no problem. Or does it?

Actually, for atheists, the problem of evil is transformed into something even worse: that nothing is evil, and, by extension, that nothing is good. For if there is no God, then "good" and "evil" are nothing more than subjective feelings that reflect what our culture has taught us to approve or disapprove, or what we individually happen to like or dislike. Hence, for atheists there is no answer to the question of evil because there is really no question. There is no such thing as evil; we are merely projecting our private feelings onto external events.

But does this satisfy the innate human outrage over evil and suffering? Of course not. Instead, it mocks us by reducing our deepest moral convictions to a trick of our minds. We may be robbed, our children may be murdered, we may die a lingering death, but none of this is genuinely evil. It is merely part of nature because nature is all that exists. We may cry out in the night for answers, but objective reality is indifferent to our tears.

On its own terms, atheism simply has no answer, and the pointlessness of our suffering makes it all the more painful.

Ironically, though, when things go horribly wrong, even diehard atheists shake their fists at heaven; even those who say God does not exist instinctively blame Him for their sorrows. There are no atheists in the foxhole, as the saying goes.

False Solution #1: Some people solve the problem of evil by _____.

Let's move to various religious answers.

Some people solve the problem of evil by casting them as illusions created by our own minds. But can anyone really live consistently with such a philosophy of denial? The story is told of a boy who went to his Christian Science practitioner and asked him to pray for his father, who was very ill. "Your father only thinks he is sick," the man told the boy. "He must learn to counter those negative thoughts and realize he is actually healthy." When the boy came back the next day, the minister asked about his father. "Today he thinks he's dead," replied the boy.

During my White House days, I personally witnessed the futility of trying to pretend evil is not real. Among President Nixon's small circle of top advisors were four Christian Scientists, including Bob Haldeman and the late John Ehrlichman, the two men closest to the president during the critical months following the Watergate break-in, when the cover-up was being fashioned. One evening during the scandal, I met with Bob Haldeman and warned him that any cover-up would imperil the presidency. The tough-minded chief of staff swung around in his chair and glared at me.

"What would you do?" he demanded.

"Don't provide any money to the burglars who broke into the Watergate offices," I suggested. "It could be considered hush money."

Haldeman brushed aside my caution with a steely gaze. "Everyone has defense funds," he said.

I kept pressing. "Bob, the president needs a good criminal defense attorney to advise him."

"Nah," Haldeman replied. "We've done nothing wrong. What he needs is just a good PR man."

With Nixon's chief advisors assuring him that his only problem was public image, he was never forced to confront reality. But the lessons of history tell us that if we do not believe in evil, we cannot cope with the reality when it hits us squarely in the face. The illusion theory simply cannot hold up under the weight of human experience.

False Solution #2: Some people solve the problem of evil by casting them as _____.

Other people solve the problem of evil by believing the idea of a remote God. Some theologians teach about a God who is so distant and transcendent that He cannot be defined by any concept in the human mind. "God is beyond good and evil," people sometimes say. This may sound lofty and reverent, but if the terms good and evil do not apply to ultimate reality, then they are mere quirks of our own subjective consciousness. The idea of God as "wholly other" makes Him so utterly transcendent that our moral outrage finds no echoing outrage in Him. We are still left alone with our tears in the night. [13]

False Solution #3: Other people solve the problem of evil by believing the _____ _____

Still other people solve the problem of sin by asserting that God is limited in His power. The reasoning here is that an all-powerful God would not allow bad things to happen; since bad things do happen, God must not be all-powerful. This perspective is gaining popularity today through a school of thought known as *process theology*, which proposes a God who is still in the process of becoming—a God who is evolving with the world and is not yet omnipotent. This God has the best of intentions (He really would like to change things), but being finite, He is not able to get rid of the evil that plagues creation. According to this view, our hope is in the future, when God and the world will reach a glorious new stage of evolution and all ills will be overcome.

False Solution #4: Still other people solve the problem of sin by _____
_____

A final group of people solve the problem of evil by suggesting that God is the omnipotent Creator but that He created a broken and evil world in order to give us choice. The notion that God created evil for purposes that are ultimately good is an obvious fallacy, for it is clear that many evil things do not lead to good results.

False Solution #5: A final group of people solve the problem of evil by suggesting that God is the omnipotent Creator but that He
_____
_____
_____

Reread these false solutions again and write why each solution is false.

#1 _____

#2 _____

#3 _____

#4 _____

#5 _____

So why is there evil in the world? How do we find any meaning in our suffering? None of the alternatives described above satisfies the cry of the human heart. Every one of them either diminishes God or diminishes us. Only the biblical explanation is consistent with both reason and human experience, for it alone tells us how God can be God—the ultimate reality and Creator of all things—and yet not be responsible for evil.

Answer the following question: "How does the Bible reconcile God's goodness and power with the presence of evil?" _____
_____
_____
_____
_____

Scripture teaches that God is good and that He created a good universe. It also teaches that the universe is now marred by evil, death, and suffering. Logically there is only one way to reconcile these two statements: There must be a source of evil outside God. And that is exactly what Scripture tells us. The decision to sin was made in the spiritual realm by Satan and the other fallen angels, who are intelligent beings capable of genuine moral choice; sin then entered our finite world through the free moral choices made by the first human beings, Adam and Eve. From there, the plague has spread through all of history because of the free moral choices humans continue to make. Evil is real, but God is not its source.

It is vital that we recognize the historicity of the Fall in the garden. Scripture gives a genuine answer to the problem of evil because it insists that God created the world good—and that sin entered at a particular point in history. And when that happened, it caused a cataclysmic change, distorting and disfiguring creation, resulting in death and destruction. That's why evil is so hateful, so repulsive, and why we cry against it in the night. Our response is entirely appropriate, and the only reason God can truly comfort us is that He's on our side. He did not create evil, and He hates the way it has disfigured His handiwork.

Consider the following questions proposed to you by a skeptical friend. How would you answer each question?

"But if God knew beforehand that we would make such a mess of things, says the skeptic, why did He let it happen?" _____
_____
_____
_____

"Why did He create us capable of sinning?"
_____
_____
_____
_____

In order for God to ensure that we could not sin, He would have to have denied us the capacity for choice—which would have rendered us less than human, incapable of creativity, moral heroism, loyalty, love, and obedience. The only way to have creatures that are fully human is to take the risk that they will use their freedom to choose evil.

Then, once humans did choose evil, God's holy character required justice. He could not ignore it, overlook it, or simply wipe the slate clean and start over again. Once the scales of justice had been tipped, they had to be balanced. Once the moral fabric of the universe had been torn, it had to be mended.

In that case, says the critic, the human race should have ended with Adam and Eve. They should have been punished for their rebellion, cast into hell, and that would have been the end of human history. Ah, but God is merciful as well as just, and He devised an astonishing alternative: He Himself would bear the punishment for His creatures. God Himself would enter the world of humanity and suffer the judgment and death that sinful humans deserved. And that is exactly what He did, through the God-man, Jesus Christ.

It is a unique solution, unlike any other attempt to solve the problem of evil. Jesus met the demands of divine justice by accepting execution on a Roman cross. How did God beat Satan at his own game? (Read Isaiah 53:5.) Through His death on the cross, Jesus defeated evil and guaranteed the ultimate victory over it. What will God do at the end of time? (Read Revelation 21:4.)

Until that time, God uses the "thorns and thistles" that have infested creation since the Fall to teach, chastise, sanctify, and transform us, making us ready for that new heaven and earth. This is something I well understand: The greatest blessings in my life have emerged from suffering, and I have seen the same process repeated in countless lives. Just as it hurts when the doctor sets a broken bone, so it can cause enormous pain when God resets our character. Yet it is the only way to be whole and healthy.

What spiritual lessons have you learned from personal examples of suffering? _____
_____
_____

An ancient document describing the martyrs of the church in the first century says that they "attained such towering strength of soul that not one of them uttered a cry or groan."[14] Through suffering, God gives all who turn to Him "towering strength of soul." Because we are fallen creatures, it often takes suffering to detach us from our wrong habits, our mistaken ideas, and the idols we live for, so that our hearts are free to love God.

In his famous doctrine of "Blessed Fault," Augustine encapsulated the mystery of suffering: "God judged it better to bring good out of evil than to suffer no evil at all."[15] Better to endure the pain involved in redeeming sinners than not to create human beings at all.

Why did He do that? There is only one answer. Love. God loved us so much that even when He foresaw the sin and suffering that would darken and distort His creation, He chose to create us anyway. That is the profoundest mystery of all, and one that inspires our hearts to worship.

Just as it hurts when the doctor sets a broken bone, so it can cause enormous pain when God resets our character. Yet it is the only way to be whole and healthy.

⬢ Points to Remember

List two key points of today's session.

1. _____
   _____

2. _____
   _____

❓ Questions to Ask

What questions do I have concerning what I've read today? _____
_____
_____
_____

👥 Actions to Take

Based on what I've read, what specific action(s) should I take? _____
_____
_____
_____

✳ Prayers to Pray

Today, God, you taught me _____
_____
_____
_____
_____
_____

Help me, Lord, to _____
_____
_____
_____
_____

NOTES

[1] William F. Buckley Jr., *Nearer My God: An Autobiography of Faith* (New York: Doubleday, 1997), 232.

[2] Jean-Jacques Rousseau, *The Social Contract* (Boston: Charles E. Tuttle, Everyman's Classic Library, 1993), 181.

[3] Rousseau, *The Social Contract*, 275.

[4] Ibid., 195.

[5] Friedrich Nietzsche, *The Birth of Tragedy and the Genealogy of Morals*, trans. Francis Golffing (New York: Doubleday, 1956), 277-78.

[6] Based on "Evolution and the Humanities," a presentation made by Willem J. Ouweneel at the National Creation Conference, August 1985.

[7] Based on "Evolution and the Humanities," a presentation made by Willem J. Ouweneel at the National Creation Conference, August 1985.

[8] B. F. Skinner, *Walden Two* (New York: Macmillan, 1976).

[9] Karl Vick, "Delaware Seeks Death Penalty against Teens in Infant's Death," *Washington Post*, 19 November 1996.

[10] Susan Wise Bauer, "Stephen King's Tragic Kingdom," *Books & Culture* (March/April 1997): 14.

[11] Nick Gillespie and Lisa Snell, "Contemplating Evil: Novelist Dean Koontz on Freud, Fraud, and the Great Society," *Reason 28*, no. 6 (November 1996): 44.

[12] Einstein, *The World As I See It*, 24-29.

[13] Paul Helm, "Faith and Reason: Stained with the Blood of Suffering," *The Independent*, 23 April 1994.

[14] *The Martyrdom of the Holy Polycarp*, as cited in Eberhard Arnold, *The Early Christians: After the Death of the Apostles* (Rifton, N.Y.: Plough, 1972), 66.

[15] Saint Augustine, *Enchiridon*, 27, as quoted in *The Book of Catholic Quotations*, ed. John Chapin (New York: Farrar, Straus and Cudahy, 1956), 313.

Can This Dilemma Be Fixed?

The result of the Fall is hard to deal with from a secular
worldview. In this session, the Fall is seen from a different
perspective with a focus on God's plan for creation.

DAY ONE
The Gift of Life's Beginning

"I praise you because I am fearfully and wonderfully made; your works are wonderful, I know that full well" (Psalm 139:14).

In 1970, when New York liberalized its abortion laws, Dr. Bernard Nathanson began running the nation's largest abortion clinic, the Center for Reproductive and Sexual Health (known to staff members by its acronym, CRASH). Located in Manhattan, the facility thrived on referrals from the Reverend Howard Moody's Clergy Consultation Service on Abortion, a network of Protestant ministers and Jewish rabbis. Nathanson took pride in the clinic's high professional standards and in the success of its outpatient surgical model.

By 1973, however, with abortion on demand as a legal procedure across the country as a result of *Roe v. Wade*, Nathanson decided to make a career change. He accepted a position as chief of obstetrical service at St. Luke's Hospital Center and went from tending mothers to tending babies (although he continued to perform abortions). His task was to organize a sophisticated perinatology unit, complete with electronic fetal-monitoring machines and other expensive equipment to treat ailing newborns.

At the time, one of the most exciting new gadgets was the ultrasound machine, which literally opened a window on fetal development. The first time Nathanson saw an ultrasound in action, he was with a group of residents gathered around a pregnant patient in a darkened examining room, watching a demonstration by a technician sent by the company to train hospital staff to use the machine.

The technician first applied a conductive gel to the woman's abdomen and then began working a handheld sensor over her stomach. As the splatter on the video screen clarified, Nathanson ·was amazed. He could see a throbbing heart! The technician focused closely on this image, and Nathanson could see all four chambers pumping. It looked like an animated blossom, with such thickness and definition that it took his breath away. He could also see the major vessels leading to and from the cardiac rose.

The technician next brought the baby's forehead, eyes, and mouth into focus. Then, by zooming out, the technician showed that the baby had its hands folded over its face. Right hand, left hand. One finger, two, three, four, and a thumb, Nathanson counted on each hand. When the baby moved its hands, Nathanson could see it sucking in amniotic fluid.

The view from above the crown of the baby's head showed the development of the brain, where the first folds could be seen. Then the technician scanned the elegant architecture of the spine. The view swung around to the back to give a glimpse of a kidney, then moved to the baby's bladder, which was full. Nathanson would later learn that early in the third trimester, a child is already evacuating, while the amniotic fluid is cleaned by the mother's placenta.

The group took a close look at the umbilical cord. Through the cord they could discern three faint lines. "Here you see two arteries leading in and one vein leading out," the technician said. "You can't often see that."

Was it a boy or a girl? Just like expectant parents, Nathanson and the others couldn't help wondering. It was a girl. Then finally, the technician showed the bone structure of the legs, and each foot with its five perfect toes.

During the course of the scan, Nathanson noticed that his mind had dropped the word fetus in favor of baby.

What do you think caused Nathanson to have these thoughts? _____
_____
_____
_____

Suddenly, all that Nathanson had been learning about the child in the womb since his entry into the field of perinatology snapped into focus. For example, he knew that a fertilized human egg becomes a self-directed entity very early, after it has multiplied into only four cells; that the heart beat begins as early as the eighteenth day after conception; that at six weeks the major organ systems have formed. In fact, after only twelve weeks, there are no new anatomical developments; the child simply grows larger and more capable of sustaining life outside the womb.

All these had been only medical facts, but now they coalesced with the grainy image on the screen and crashed into Nathanson's consciousness. He felt a chill along his spine, and the air in the room seemed to grow denser, making it hard for him to breathe, making him want to bolt. His mood swung from the exaltation of new knowledge to a brow-sweating panic as the question hit him: How many babies just like this little girl had he himself sliced up? How many human lives had he taken?

We'll get back to Nathanson in our next session, but it's now time for your midterm exam!

You may know about the birds and the bees (we'll get to that subject soon) but do you know what happens after conception? Take this quick quiz to find out how much you do know about the first nine months of your life.[1]

1. You started swimming and doing back flips when your mom was:
(A) 6 months pregnant
(B) 9 weeks
(C) 8 months
(D) Forget the back flips, you can't even do a good belly-flop.

2. If you kept growing all nine months as fast as you did during your second month, you would have been born as big as:
(A) Arnold Schwarzenegger
(B) An M-1 tank
(C) A pair of overfed elephants

3. When did you most likely feel pain for the first time?
(A) When they cut your umbilical cord
(B) When your mom was 7 weeks pregnant
(C) After a big lunch in a cafeteria

4. By the time your mother found out she was pregnant, you were:
(A) A tiny speck smaller than the period at the end of a sentence
(B) A miniature human with arms, legs and a heartbeat
(C) A ball of cells the size of a marble

5. Your mother says you started to kick and poke her:
(A) 3 months into the pregnancy
(B) At 4 months
(C) Never mind when you started, when are you going to stop?

6. Five months into the pregnancy you got a lot of hiccups because:
(A) Your mom was pigging out on pickles, ice cream, pizza and sardines.
(B) You swallowed amniotic fluid.
(C) Your diaphragm was being formed.

(Quiz continued on next page)

(D) You couldn't find a bag to put over your head.

7. Before you were born, your skin was:
(A) As wrinkled as a California Raisin
(B) As waxy as a statue from Ripley's Believe It or Not museum
(C) Both of the above

8. When did you start using your brain?
(A) When your mom was 8 months pregnant
(B) When she was 40 days pregnant
(C) If you still haven't started using your brain, go on to the next question.

9. When was the color of your hair determined?
(A) At conception
(B) 3 months into the pregnancy
(C) Only your hairdresser knows for sure

10. Five months before you were born, your heart pumped enough blood every day to:
(A) Overflow a coffee mug
(B) Fill half a tank of a Firebird
(C) Fill an olympic size swimming pool

11. When did you first start looking like either a boy or a girl?
(A) The seventh month of pregnancy
(B) The end of the second month
(C) When the doctor announced to your parents, "It's a..."

12. If your mother smoked while she was pregnant, you may have been born:
(A) Overweight and overdue
(B) Underweight and premature
(C) With yellow teeth and a nagging cough

13. How premature can a baby be born and still survive?
(A) 4 weeks early
(B) 8 weeks early
(C) 16 weeks early

14. When did you begin to look like your mom and dad?
(A) When your mom was 6 months pregnant
(B) When your mom was 4 months pregnant
(C) Who cares when it happened—does anybody know a good plastic surgeon?

ANSWERS TO QUIZ QUESTIONS

1. B. At nine weeks you could swim a mean backstroke. Your favorite technique was a little backwards walk, leading with your head.
2. C. It's a good thing you slowed down after the second month, or your birthweight would've been 14 tons. Let Daddy try bouncing that on his knee!
3. B. By seven weeks all the structures necessary for pain sensation are functioning. You would try your hardest to avoid the source of pain.
4. B. About eight weeks after conception, all systems were go: skeletal, nervous, digestive, circulatory and respiratory. The only job left was to refine what you already had.
5. B. At only a couple of months you started to shake, rattle and roll, but you were too little for mom to notice. By four or five months, however, she swore you had a black belt in karate.
6. B. Not only does amniotic fluid make a cushy "water-bed," but it's also full of glucose (sugar). Swallowing the fluid was good practice for your digestive system and made for a healthier baby.
7. C. About half way through the pregnancy, you had lots of nice skin but not much fat to fill it out. That's why premature babies look wrinkled—they need more "meat on their bones." The wax-works effect was caused by the vernix, a thick whitish cream which covered your skin to protect it from the amniotic fluid.
8. B. Fetal electric brain waves have been traced as early as the sixth week. What do you suppose you were thinking about?
9. A. At conception, each parent contributed approximately 50,000 chemical "instruction sheets" (genes) that determined not only what you look like, but also your health, talents, tastes, athletic abilities, intelligence, allergies, and more.
10. B. Four months after conception you were pumping six gallons of blood each day through a body about as long as your hand is now. And it was your blood, not your mothers—you never shared her circulatory system. You may even have a completely different blood type!
11. B. You were either male or female from the point of conception, but it took about 46 days for parts to be recognized. Thanks to modern science, parents can now see the sex of their unborn baby with the help of an ultrasound machine by about four months. At last, they can answer the age-old question: "What color should I paint the nursery?"
12. B. A smoking mom sends nicotine, carbon monoxide, carbonic acid and wood alcohol right down the line to her baby. Smoking two packs a day reduces a baby's birth weight by 10%—which can seriously reduce the infant's chances of survival.
13. C. With modern technology, babies as young as 22 weeks after conception, weighing only 14 oz., have survived premature birth. You would need a lot of medical help, but would fight like a champion to hold on to life.
14. B. During your fourth month, you grew to the grand height of eight inches and began to resemble your parents. At ten weeks you had a unique trait that may interest the FBI someday—fingerprints. Nobody ever had or will have the same set.

Turn to Psalm 139 and answer the following questions.

1. Why does the psalmist praise God?
_____
_____

2. What does the psalmist say about the presence of God in His universe?
_____
_____

3. What is God's involvement with a child in his mother's womb? _____
_____
_____

4. What personal request does the psalmist ask of God at the close of this chapter?
_____
_____

✔ Points to Remember
List two key points of today's session.
1. _____
_____
2. _____
_____

❓ Questions to Ask
What questions do I have concerning what I've read today? _____

_____
_____
_____

👥 Actions to Take
Based on what I've read, what specific action(s) should I take? _____
_____
_____
_____
_____

✳ Prayers to Pray
Today, God, you taught me _____
_____
_____
_____
_____
_____

Help me, Lord, to _____
_____
_____
_____
_____

DAY TWO
Abstract Concepts Becoming Vivid Images

"Create in me a pure heart, O God, and renew a steadfast spirit within me" (Psalm 51:10).

Back to Dr. Bernard Nathanson . . . One day, Nathanson had a brainstorm. If ultrasound could reveal the baby in the womb, it could also be used to witness an abortion. He asked a colleague who was performing many abortions a day to put an ultrasound device on a few of the patients and tape the procedures, all with the patient's permission.

Nathanson knew very well what hap-

Bernard
Nathanson
realized he had
learned one over-
whelming lesson
from his father,
who was a doctor
driven by materi-
alism: Don't let
anyone get in
your way.

pened in an abortion. Yet when abstract concepts were transformed into vivid images—when he saw tiny bodies being torn limb from limb—he was startled and revolted. But what truly sickened him was something completely unexpected: The ultrasound showed the babies responding to the abortion process. One tape showed a twelve-week fetus desperately trying to wriggle away from the suction apparatus. The fetus continued to struggle even after it had been severely maimed, opening his mouth in what looked like a scream of fear and pain, though, of course, the ultrasound recorded no sound.

At the same time, an internal "silent scream" began to dominate Nathanson's life. He repeatedly asked himself: Why had I been so completely blind to the true nature of abortion? How could I have presided over mass slaughter with such a crassly utilitarian attitude, reducing it to a matter of professional competence in performing a medical procedure?

Consider that Nathanson had just proposed these questions to you. What response would you have given him?

1. _____
   _____
2. _____
   _____

He began a profound examination of conscience, digging into his past to uncover the source of his skewed ideas. Bernard Nathanson realized he had learned one overwhelming lesson from his father, who was a doctor driven by materialism: *Don't let anyone get in your way.*

And he had learned the lesson well, consigning not one, but two of his own children to death. The first time an unwanted pregnancy threatened to "get in the way," he was in medical school, and he gave his pregnant lover the money to get an illegal abortion. The second time was in the mid-sixties, when he was between marriages

and his womanizing resulted in an inconvenient pregnancy. He performed that abortion himself.

Years later, after much reflection, the worst moral baggage burdening Nathanson was abortion. Abortion, abortion, abortion. How ironic that his one great humanitarian cause turned out to be nothing less than mass slaughter. Bernard Nathanson had come face-to-face with guilt. Real guilt. Not a passing feeling of shame or a confused embarrassment, but a brutal, crushing, dogged knowledge of his own evil. He was, in his own words, "a charred ruin."[2]

Off and on during the late 1980s, Nathanson contemplated suicide. He would awake from fitful dreams at four or five o'clock in the morning, feeling as if he were being strangled by some nameless dread. His grandfather and sister had committed suicide, and he found himself asking, "Would the people closest to me find my death a relief?"

He turned to what he called the "literature of sin." He read St. Augustine's *Confessions* repeatedly and absorbed books by Kierkegaard, Tillich, Niebuhr, and Dostoyevsky—works that described the soul's tormented search for answers to guilt. "How long," Augustine wrote, "will I insist on pursuing the maddening desires that have brought me so much unhappiness? Will I ever truly desire deliverance?"[3] Augustine wanted to turn to God, but he couldn't bring himself to do it. Nathanson's own cry echoed Augustine's agonizing meditations.

"I felt the burden of sin growing heavier and more insistent," Nathanson wrote. "I *had* such heavy moral baggage to drag into the next world. . . . I *was* afraid."[4]

Check the appropriate response to each statement.

1. I struggle with guilt in my own life.
❏ Always ❏ Often ❏ Sometimes
❏ Rarely ❏ Never

2. I have had a history of being unhappy.
❑ Always ❑ Often ❑ Sometimes
❑ Rarely ❑ Never

3. God has forgiven me of my past sins.
❑ Always ❑ Often ❑ Sometimes
❑ Rarely ❑ Never

4. I have found peace in my relationship with Christ.
❑ Always ❑ Often ❑ Sometimes
❑ Rarely ❑ Never

5. My relationship with Christ gives me comfort and hope.
❑ Always ❑ Often ❑ Sometimes
❑ Rarely ❑ Never

Then, in 1989, Nathanson attended a pro-life rally in New York City to gather data for an article he was writing on the ethics of abortion clinic protests. Forbidden to participate himself because of a court order stemming from earlier protests where he had been convicted of trespassing, he stood apart as an objective observer. And what he saw finally broke through his defenses.

The pro-life activists seemed to have an otherworldly peace. "With pro-choicers hurling the most fulsome epithets at them, the police surrounding them, the media openly unsympathetic to their cause, the federal judiciary fining and jailing them, and municipal officials threatening them— all through it they sat smiling, quietly praying, singing, confident." They exhibited an "intensity of love and prayer that astonished me."

It was only then, with this vivid image of love pressing on him, that Nathanson began "for the first time in my entire adult life . . . to entertain seriously the notion of God."[5]

Almost immediately, he turned from the literature of sin to the literature of conversion, especially to *Pillar of Fire,* written by Karl Stern, one of Nathanson's former teachers who had been the leading figure in McGill University's department of psychiatry. Now, reading Stern's account of his own conversion, Nathanson realized for the first time why his former teacher had exerted such a striking effect on him. In his book, Stern described his long intellectual journey from nominal Judaism to a highly intellectual and devout Christianity. In retrospect, Nathanson realized that Stern's religious beliefs were what had transformed mere medical technique into medical care.

That's the kind of transformation I want in my own life and practice, he thought.

Can you recall a professor who has demonstrated Christianity by how or what he/she taught? In what way(s) was this evident to you? _____
_____
_____

In 1993, Nathanson shut down his practice to pursue advanced studies in bioethics, first at Georgetown University then at Vanderbilt University, where bioethics students were allowed to incorporate religious studies in their programs. It was here he began asking, how can one know forgiveness personally and individually? How could he himself be delivered from death–the death of all the lives he had taken and the death of his own soul?

In the wee hours of the morning he sometimes felt that he had already entered a hell marked "No Exit," that his "good intentions" had led him to become, in his words, the "Mayor of Hell."[6] His own sense of justice haunted him. He stood condemned in his own eyes. Was there any hope for him? Our study of Psalm 51 will address this question.

What can you personally do?

Pray[7]

Pray for the women who are this very moment in the midst of a crisis pregnancy. Pray that God's Spirit would give these

How can one know forgiveness personally and individually? How could he himself be delivered from death—the death of all the lives he had taken and the death of his own soul?

women and those around them the discernment to choose life.

Pray for the millions who have had abortions and their families as they now deal with the trauma from those decisions. Pray that they would bring their pain and suffering to the foot of the cross and know that Christ is able and willing to forgive them for this transgression.

Act

Educate yourself about sanctity of human life issues, such as euthanasia and assisted suicide, cloning and genetic research, and abortion, and what the Bible says about these issues.

Contact a local Crisis Pregnancy Center to determine if you can assist them in their ministry by sponsoring a "baby shower" for the center, provide needed items of clothing for expectant mothers or newborns, or train to be a labor coach for single mothers-to-be.

For further study, check out these organizations:
National Right to Life: www.nrlc.org
Pro-life resources: www.prolife.org

America's Crisis Pregnancy Helpline:
(toll-free) 1-888-4OPTIONS
(888-467-8466) www.thehelpline.org

The Elliott Institute (post-abortion):
www.afterabortion.org

ERLC (educational resources):
(1-800-475-9125) www.erlc.com

Know

It is difficult to fully comprehend the preciousness of human life without considering what God has done to provide a way for us to fellowship with Him. God loved you so much—knowing you even before you were born—that He sent His Son to die a torturous death on a cross for your sake. In accepting His Son as your Lord and Savior,

your sins will be forgiven and eternal life will be yours. He loves you that much.

How can you know Jesus Christ? Read the following Scriptures for the answer to this question. Beside each Scripture rewrite the verse in your own words.

Isaiah 64:6 _____
_____
_____
_____

Romans 3:23 _____
_____

Romans 10:13 _____
_____

Romans 5:8 _____
_____
_____

John 3:16 _____
_____
_____

Turn to Psalm 51 and answer the following questions.

What has God done which allows us to be able to ask Him to forgive us our sins? _____
_____
_____
_____

What does David say he will do after recovering "the joy of your salvation"? _____
_____
_____
_____

What are "the sacrifices of God?" _____
_____
_____
_____
_____
_____

Points to Remember

List two key points of today's session.

1. _____
   _____
2. _____
   _____

Questions to Ask

What questions do I have concerning what I've read today? _____
_____
_____
_____

Actions to Take

Based on what I've read, what specific action(s) should I take? _____
_____
_____

Prayers to Pray

Today, God, you taught me _____
_____
_____
_____
_____
_____
_____
_____
_____
_____

Help me, Lord, to _____
_____
_____
_____
_____
_____
_____
_____

DAY THREE
Seeing Deliverance

"For the love of money is a root of all kinds of evil. Some people, eager for money, have wandered from the faith and pierced themselves with many griefs" (1 Timothy 6:10).

One day in late autumn 1996, my secretary informed me of a surprising phone call. Dr. Bernard Nathanson was inviting my wife and me to his baptism at St. Patrick's Cathedral, and Cardinal John O'Connor would be presiding.

I was stunned. "Are you sure you've got the right name?" I asked. "Bernard Nathanson?"

"That's it," she smiled.

I had known that Nathanson was interested in Christianity; in fact, the two of us had been trying to meet for some time, but we had been unable to coordinate our schedules. Although I confess my initial disappointment that I hadn't introduced him to my Baptist tradition, the news that the man who was once the nation's leading abortionist was a Christian made this an invitation I couldn't refuse.

It was a striking moment of spiritual victory. Most of the time, Christians fight in the trenches, seeing only the bloody warfare around us. But every so often God permits us a glimpse of the real victory. This was one of those wonderful, rare, illuminating moments, as we watched Bernie Nathanson—a Jew by birth, a man who had been an atheist by conviction, a brilliant doctor who had been amoral by profession—kneeling before the cross of Christ.

Bernard Nathanson had been redeemed.

This was one of those wonderful, rare, illuminating moments, as we watched Bernie Nathanson—a Jew by birth, a man who had been an atheist by conviction, a brilliant doctor who had been amoral by profession—kneeling before the cross of Christ.

Just as every worldview offers an answer to the question of how we got here (creation), and an analysis of the basic human dilemma (the Fall), so every worldview offers a way to solve that dilemma (redemption).

He was a new man, taking his first tentative steps into a new world of faith and hope, his fears relieved, his tormented soul transformed, and the most vexing questions of life answered.

Not all of us, of course, are driven to the depths of despair that Bernie Nathanson was. Yet all human beings yearn, deep in their hearts, for deliverance from sin and guilt, for freedom and meaning. Many try to suppress the longing, to rationalize it away, to mute it with lesser answers. But ultimately, it is impossible to evade. This is the great human predicament: Sooner or later, even the most decent among us know that there is a rottenness at our core. We all long to find freedom from our guilt and failures, to find some greater meaning and purpose in life, to know that there is hope.

This need for salvation has been imprinted on the human soul since the first couple went astray in the garden.

In your own words, describe the redemption Christ offers to us. _____
_____
_____
_____
_____

But religions and philosophies are not the only ones offering redemption. Any belief system in the marketplace of ideas, any movement that attracts followers, anything that has the power to grab people's hearts and win their allegiance does so because it taps into their deepest longings. And those longings are, ultimately, religious.

Just as every worldview offers an answer to the question of how we got here (creation), and an analysis of the basic human dilemma (the Fall), so every worldview offers a way to solve that dilemma (redemption).

Write an appropriate question beside each word below. (If you have trouble, reread the paragraph above.)

Creation: _____
_____

Fall: _____
_____

Redemption: _____
_____

But Which Offer of Redemption Is True?

Which gives a genuine answer to the human dilemma? And which are crass counterfeits?

The siren that calls many people today is the one that claimed Bernie Nathanson's heart and soul for so long: the belief that the object of life is material, that achievement and advancement and sensual pleasure are "all there is." And America has a highly developed, technologically advanced industry—the advertising industry—designed to entice us with redemption promised through materialism and commercialism.

Every time we turn on the television set or open a magazine or newspaper, we are bombarded with the message that for every need, every insecurity, every worry is a product that can satisfy that need, pump up that self-esteem, soothe those worries.

And since these deepest needs are religious, what ads really trade on is the universal longing for redemption.

List three commercials you have seen with this type message.
1. _____
_____
2. _____
_____
3. _____
_____

This message takes various forms. Sometimes ads trade on themes of personal faith, with slogans such as, "I found it!" "It's the right thing." "Something to believe in." Others offer a veiled substitute for a personal relationship with the divine: "Me and my R.C." "You're in good hands." Still others suggest the blessings of the Promised Land: "We bring good things to life." "Be all you can be." Finally, some ads exploit the rhetoric of religious gratitude: "Thank you, Tasty-Cakes." "Thanks, Delco." "I love what you do for me."[8]

What do you feel these commercials communicate? _____
_____
_____

In short, advertisers are clearly attuned to the human yearning for salvation—and eager to exploit it.

Complete the following open-ended sentences with the first thought that comes to your mind.
To me, money is_____
The more money I have,_____
Money and happiness will_____
Success and wealth can_____
If money's my god, then_____
What God gives me He expects_____

Calvin Coolidge, our thirtieth president, once told the American Association of Advertising Agencies that "Advertising ministers to the spiritual side of trade." It is part of the "greater work of the regeneration and redemption of mankind."[9] Regeneration? Redemption? Through advertising, the "religion" of appetite and ego gratification is offered to us as a solution to the human dilemma, a comfort in our insecurities, a way of salvation. The most advanced tools of communication and persuasion are being used to press us into the service of America's most popular deity, the idol of commercialism.

Think about and jot down three ways you have been influenced by "the idol of commercialism."
1. _____
_____

2. _____
_____
3. _____
_____

Practicing the religion of consumerism is like drinking salt water: The more you drink, the thirstier you get—and finally, you die. There is never enough wealth and power to satisfy, never enough material possessions to blot out guilt. And no matter how pleasant or attractive such things can make our brief existence here on earth, they cannot carry us beyond. For the old adage is apt: You can't take it with you.

Sadly, though, while commercialism is America's favorite substitute religion, it is not the only one. Others have proven equally seductive and even more destructive.

Turn to 1 Timothy 6:1-16 and answer the following questions.

What does Timothy say about the person "who teaches false doctrines"? _____
_____
_____
_____
_____

What does Timothy say about contentment?
_____
_____
_____
_____

What can happen to a person who is "eager for money"? _____
_____
_____
_____

Rather than loving money, what does God encourage us to do? _____
_____
_____

✅ Points to Remember
List two key points of today's session.

1. _____

_____

2. _____

_____

❓ Questions to Ask
What questions do I have concerning what I've read today? _____

_____

_____

_____

👥 Actions to Take
Based on what I've read, what specific action(s) should I take? _____

_____

_____

✳ Prayers to Pray
Today, God, you taught me _____

_____

_____

_____

_____

Help me, Lord, to _____

_____

_____

_____

_____

_____

_____

_____

_____

_____

DAY FOUR
Absolute Autonomy

"And are justified freely by his grace through the redemption that came by Christ Jesus" (Romans 3:24).

When Diane went off to college, she also went off the deep end. Within weeks she was smoking pot, flouting her childhood faith, and mouthing slogans about women's liberation.

Today, Diane has returned to her Christian faith and no longer calls herself a feminist. "I got tired of being a victim," she explains. "I used to read feminist books by the armload. Then one day it hit me. All those books were the same! Every problem a woman might have was explained by saying that someone, somewhere had done her wrong—as if women were weak, passive creatures. It was pathetic."

Diane has changed her mind, but millions still march behind the banner of women's liberation—along with a host of other liberation ideologies. Across the nation, groups gather around ideologies of gender, race, and sexual orientation, seething with rage over alleged oppressions of one kind or another.

To understand the appeal these groups exert, we need to understand their underlying worldview. According to these groups, what is the human dilemma, the source of suffering and injustice?

Give your answer for each group.
Gender: _____

Race: _____

Sexual Orientation: _____

Answer: Oppression by whites or males or heterosexuals or some other group. What would you say is the solution, the way to justice and peace? _____

_____

_____

The answer is to raise our consciousness and rise up against the oppressor. Thus, the promise of liberation is ultimately a promise of redemption.

All the liberation ideologies in the marketplace of ideas today are variations on a single theme that has been pervasive in Western thought since the nineteenth century: that history is moving forward toward a glorious consummation. This is sometimes dubbed the "myth of progress," or, in the words of British philosopher Mary Midgley, "*the Escalator Myth,*" and it is a secularization of the Christian teaching of divine providence. Whereas Christianity teaches that history is moving toward the kingdom of God, the Escalator Myth reassures us that we are evolving toward an earthly utopia that is the product of human effort and ingenuity.[10]

Marxism is best understood as a prime example of the Escalator Myth—of an effort by the modern mind to secularize the kingdom of God, to create a purely human heaven here on earth.

Summarize the Escalator Myth below.

_____

_____

_____

In contrast to this myth, what does Christianity teach?

1. _____
2. _____
3. _____
4. _____

The politically correct campus today offers countless variations on the Marxist theme, but the common core of all these variations is revealed by the way they overlap and complement one another. The University of California at Santa Barbara offers a course listed as Black Marxism, linking Marxism and black liberation. Brown University connects black and homosexual liberation in a course called Black Lavender: Study of Black Gay/Lesbian Plays. UCLA relates Hispanic ethnicity with homosexuality in a course listed as Chicana Lesbian Literature. Villanova combines feminism with environmentalism in a course titled Eco-feminism. And Stanford University mixes everything in a single cauldron with a course its catalog lists as Women of Color: The Intersection of Race, Ethnicity, Class, and Gender. As a result of this massive politicization of education, college students are being taught to apply Marxist categories to law, politics, education, family studies, and many other fields.

Check the catalog at your college to see if a course with a Marxist theme is offered. If so, give a brief description of the course below.

_____

_____

While Karl Marx hunched over his books in the British Museum in the mid-nineteenth century, feverishly philosophizing, what he eventually came up with was a full-blown alternative religion. In the beginning was a creator: namely, matter itself. In Marxism the universe is a self-originating, self-operating machine, generating its own power and running by its own internal force toward a final goal—the classless, communistic society. Marx's disciple, Lenin, stated the doctrine in explicitly religious language: "We may regard the material and cosmic world as the supreme being, as the cause of all causes, as the creator of heaven and earth." [11]

According to Lenin, what is "the supreme being"? _____

The Escalator Myth reassures us that we are evolving toward an earthly utopia that is the product of human effort and ingenuity.[10]

Marxism is best understood as a prime example of the Escalator Myth—of an effort by the modern mind to secularize the kingdom of God, to create a purely human heaven here on earth.

Marxism's counterpart to the garden of Eden is the state of primitive communism. And the original sin was the creation of private property and the division of labor, which caused humanity to fall from its early state of innocence into slavery and oppression. From this follow all the subsequent evils of exploitation and class struggle.

According to Marxism, what was "the original sin"? _____

_____

The Day of Judgment, in Marxist theology, is the day of revolution, when the evil bourgeoisie will be damned. It is significant that Marx called not for repentance but for revolution. Why? Because, like Rousseau, he regarded humanity as inherently good. He believed that evil and greed arise from the economic structures of society (private property), and therefore they can be eliminated by a social revolution that destroys the old economic system and institutes a new one.

Finally, like all religions, Marxism has an eschatology (a doctrine of the final events of history).

In Christianity, the end of time is when the original perfection of God's creation will be restored, and sin and pain will be no more. In Marxism, the end of history is when the original communism will be restored and class conflict will be no more. Paradise will be ushered in by the efforts of human beings whose consciousness has been raised. Marx looked forward to this inevitable consummation of history as eagerly as any Christian anticipates the Second Coming.

Concerning the end times, place a cross beside the events which represent Christianity and an "X" besides the events which represent Marxism.
____ **Paradise will be ushered in by the efforts of human beings.**
____ **Pain will be no more.**
____ **Original perfection of God's creation will be restored.**
____ **Original communism will be restored.**
____ **Class conflict will be no more.**
____ **Sin will be no more.**

"Marxism is a secularized vision of the kingdom of God," writes theology professor Klaus Bockmuehl. "It is the kingdom of man. The race will at last undertake to create for itself that 'new earth in which righteousness dwells.'"[12] Marxism promises to solve the human dilemma and create the New Man living in an ideal society.

Marx's ultimate goal was autonomy. He was determined to become his own master, a god to himself.

This is the root of Marxism, and it is the point where we must begin to critique it. How plausible is this insistence on absolute autonomy? Ironically, Marx himself admitted that it is highly implausible. Belief in a creator, he acknowledged, is "very difficult to dislodge from popular consciousness"; at the same time, to most people the notion of absolute autonomy is "incomprehensible." Why? "Because it contradicts everything *tangible* in practical life."[13] In other words, in real life it is obvious that we are not completely autonomous. We do not create ourselves, and we cannot exist completely on our own. We are finite, contingent, dependent beings—tiny specks within a vast universe, a mere eddy within the ever flowing stream of history.

The conclusion is that Marx's worldview is fatally flawed; it does not match up with reality. And Marx himself admitted as much in acknowledging that his philosophy "contradicts everything" in "practical life."

How is Marx a living example of the apostle Paul's description of unbelievers? Read Romans 1:18-32 and write your response below. _____

_____

_____

Marxism is a substitute religion that wreaks devastation and death. And today's liberation movements, which depend heavily on the Marxist worldview, are inherently religious as well. They may have dropped Marx's focus on economics in favor of race or gender or ethnicity, but the basic thought forms remain the same—and they are equally flawed and dangerous.

Turn to Romans 3 and answer the following questions.

What do we deserve when we reject God's love? _____
_____

What does Paul say about our sinful nature?
_____
_____
_____

Paul writes that "righteousness from God" comes from what? _____
_____

What does Christ's redemption mean for us?
_____
_____

✅ **Points to Remember**
List two key points of today's session.
1. _____
_____
2. _____
_____

❓ **Questions to Ask**
What questions do I have concerning what I've read today? _____
_____
_____

👥 **Actions to Take**
Based on what I've read, what specific action(s) should I take? _____
_____
_____
_____

✳ **Prayers to Pray**
Today, God, you taught me _____
_____
_____

Help me, Lord, to _____

DAY FIVE
The Extent of Sexuality

"You were bought at a price. Therefore honor God with your body" (1 Corinthians 6:20).

Let's begin today's session with an understanding of key words and phrases dealing with sex education. Use the list of words and phrases below and write each one beside its correct definition. (abortion, adultery, AIDS, conception, fornication, homosexual, incest, intercourse, pornography, premarital intercourse, sanctity of human life)

1. _____: a phrase used primarily by Southern Baptists, based on biblical teachings, to provide a moral basis for opposition to abortion.
2. _____: the union of male and female in which the penis is inserted into the vagina.
3. _____: the union of the female ovum with the male sperm which

Margaret Sanger (1879-1966)

Margaret Sanger was born on September 14, 1879 in Corning, New York to Michael Hennessey Higgins, an Irish-born stonemason. The sixth of eleven children, Margaret blamed her mother's premature death on her frequent pregnancies. Margaret became famous as a crusader for birth-control. In keeping with her private views on sexual liberation, she had a series of affairs with several men, including Havelock Ellis and H.G. Wells.

produces an embryo that normally will grow into a baby.

4. _____: sexual intercourse between persons so closely related that they are forbidden by law to marry.

5. _____: termination of pregnancy before the fetus is capable of survival as an individual.

6. _____: human sexual intercourse other than between a man and his wife.

7. _____: acquired immune deficiency syndrome is a disease caused by a virus that destroys a person's defenses against infection.

8. _____: a person who regularly desires and seeks sexual relations with persons of the same sex.

9. _____: the portrayal of nudity or sexual activity with the primary purpose of arousing sexual desire, usually for the profit of the producer.

10. _____: voluntary sexual intercourse between a married person and someone other than his or her spouse.

11. _____: sexual intercourse between partners before marriage.

(1=sanctity of human life; 2=intercourse; 3=conception; 4=incest; 5=abortion; 6=fornication; 7=AIDS; 8=homosexual; 9=pornography; 10=adultery; 11=premarital intercourse)

Sex is a vital part of God's created order, a sacred part of the marriage covenant; and our sexual nature is a good gift from God. For many modern thinkers, sexuality became the basis for an entire worldview, the source of ultimate meaning and healing, a means of redemption. Sex was exalted into the means of raising ourselves to the next level of evolution, creating a new kind of human nature and an advanced civilization. In short, sex was tied to another form of the Escalator Myth.

Margaret Sanger pioneered the approach of understanding sexuality on a scientific level. Though generally remembered as an early champion of birth control, Sanger actually taught a much broader philosophy of sexuality, a philosophy buttressed by science. She contended that science had proved that sexual restraint suppresses the activity of the sex glands and thus injures health and dulls the intellect. The drama of history, she concluded, consists of the struggle to free our bodies and minds from the constraints of morality, the prohibitions that distort and impoverish human nature.

Work through the following situation . . .

You are a college professor who has just received a one page report on Margaret Sanger from one of your students. Your student idolizes Sanger. The following three paragraphs are the report. As a Christian, you want to challenge your students to think through, for themselves, what they write.

Margaret Sanger adamantly opposed "the 'moralists' who preached abstinence, self-denial, and suppression," and described Christian ethics as "the cruel morality of self-denial and 'sin.'" She hoped to replace it with her own morality of sexual liberation, promising that the release of sexual energies was "the only method" by which a person can find "inner peace and security and beauty." It was also the only method for overcoming social ills: "Remove the constraints and prohibitions which now hinder the release of inner energies, [and] most of the larger evils of society will perish."[14]

What Sanger offered was a "doctrine of salvation" in which morality is the root of all evil and free sexual expression is the path to redemption. She even resorted to religious language, calling on a sexual elite to "remove the moral taboos that now bind the human body and spirit, free the individual from the slavery of tradition, and above all answer their unceasing cries for knowledge that would make possible their self-direction and salvation."[15] Salvation? In another passage, she promises that men and women will literally become geniuses through "the removal of physiological and psychological inhibitions and constraints which makes possible the release and channeling of the primordial inner energies of man into full and divine expression."[16] Divine? Here's a new twist on the serpent's promise in Eden: It's not the tree in the garden; it's the release of sexual energies that will make us godlike.

This is simply another version of the Escalator Fallacy, in which sexual freedom is the means for transforming human nature and creating the New Man.

What are the strengths and weaknesses of what you just read? _____
_____
_____
_____
_____

One of Sanger's contemporaries, Alfred Kinsey, was equally influential in shaping sexual mores and sex-education theories.

To liberate sex from morality, Kinsey reduced sex to the sheer biological act of physical orgasm. He then claimed that all orgasms are morally equivalent—whether between married or unmarried persons, between people of the same or the opposite sex, between adults or children, even between humans and animals. His model was the animal world. Kinsey was a devout Darwinian and believed that since humans evolved from animals, there are no significant differences between them. He liked to talk about "the human animal," and if a particular behavior could be found among animals, he made it normative for humans as well. For example, Kinsey claimed that certain mammals are observed to have sexual contact between males, and even across species; therefore, he concluded,

both homosexuality and bestiality are "part of the normal mammalian picture" and are acceptable behavior for humans.[17]

Summarize Kinsey's views on sex as given here. _____
_____
_____
_____
_____

Along with Sanger and Kinsey, another major influence was Austrian psychologist Wilhelm Reich, who became something of a cult figure in the 1960s. His contribution was the search for the "ultimate orgasm," which quickly became one of the fads of the human potential movement. Reich believed that human beings are nothing more than biological creatures and that redemption comes through complete immersion in the sexual reflex.

Reich's ideas were incorporated by Robert Rimmer in his provocative novel *The Harrad Experiment*, published in 1966. The book sold three million copies and helped fuel the sexual revolution. For an entire generation of college-educated Americans, it became recommended reading in college courses on marriage and family, and many people credit the book with being instrumental in the sudden merger of male colleges with female colleges and in the creation of coed dormitories.

Summarize Reich's views on sex. _____
_____
_____
_____
_____

Clearly sexuality is being presented as more than mere sensual gratification or titillation. It is nothing less than a form of redemption, a means to heal the fundamental flaw in human nature. Only when we see these sexual ideologies as complete worldviews, held with the fervor of a reli-

Alfred Kinsey (1894-1956)

Alfred Charles Kinsey, a Harvard-trained professor of zoology at Indiana University established his academic reputation in studies of evolution. In 1938, he was asked to coordinate a course for students who were married or contemplating marriage. The course led to the founding of the "Institute for Sex Research." In *Kinsey: Crimes and Consequences* Dr. Judith Reisman revealed that Kinsey sexually abused infants and young boys as research for his 1948 report.

Wilhelm Reich (1897-1957)

Austrian psychoanalyst and biophysicist Wilhelm Reich was born in 1897. Once associated with Austrian psychoanalyst Sigmund Freud, Reich immigrated to the United States and advocated his theory of an orgone energy. He believed that this energy permeates the universe and that humans must release it through sexual activity to avoid developing neuroses.

gion, will we understand why Christians and moral conservatives find it so hard to change sex-education courses in public schools. You won't find contemporary sex educators using words like salvation; nonetheless, many hold the same basic assumption that free sexual expression is the means to a full and healthy life.

Recall, for a moment, the approach your elementary, junior high, and high school took in sex education. Summarize the messages taught to you through these courses. (Review some of the key words and phrases at the beginning of today's session.) _____

_____

_____

_____

_____

_____

Read the following Scriptures and write a brief summary statement of each.
Genesis 1:27-28 _____

_____

Genesis 2:15-25 _____

_____

Deuteronomy 6:4-9 _____

_____

Joshua 24:15 _____

_____

Proverbs 5:15-19 _____

_____

Romans 1:26-27 _____

_____

_____

Mary Calderone, a major architect of contemporary sex education and former executive director of Sex Information and Education of the United States (SIECUS), believes that human nature is not evolving as quickly as technology. She feels that we must remold human nature itself to fit the modern, ever-changing world. A new stage of evolution is breaking across the horizon, she writes, and the task of educators is to prepare children to step into that new world. To do this, they must pry children away from old views and values, especially from biblical and other traditional forms of sexual morality—for "religious laws or rules about sex were made on the basis of ignorance of facts now known."[18]

Summarize Calderone's views on sex. _____

_____

_____

_____

When we trace the history of ideas about sexuality, it becomes clear that the founders of sex education never did seek simply to transmit a collection of facts about how our bodies work. Rather, they were evangelists for a utopian worldview, a religion, in which a "scientific" understanding of sexuality is the means for transforming human nature, freeing it from the constraints of morality and ushering in an ideal society. It is another form of the Escalator Myth.

Yet if we examine the lives of these self-appointed prophets, we find little grounds for believing their grandiose promises. Margaret Sanger was married twice and was involved in numerous affairs—or had, as she put it, "voluntary mates"—which became increasingly tawdry as she aged. She was addicted to the painkiller Demerol and was obsessed with numerology, astrology, and psychics in a desperate attempt to find meaning. The sexual liberation that Sanger actually lived out was not the high road to salvation that she had promised in her writing.

Kinsey, too, had a secret life we rarely hear about. His goal was "to create his own sexual utopia," says biographer Jones, and Kinsey built up a select circle of friends and colleagues who committed themselves to

92   How Now Shall We Live? Collegiate Edition

his philosophy of total sexual freedom. Since the results were often captured on film, we know that Kinsey and his wife both had sexual relations with a host of male and female staff members and other people. Kinsey was a homosexual and a masochist, sometimes engaging in bizarre and painful practices.[19]

But Kinsey had an even darker secret. In *Kinsey, Sex, and Fraud*, scientist Judith Reisman argues convincingly that Kinsey's research on child sexual responses could have been obtained only if he, or his colleagues, were actually engaged in the sexual molestation of children. How else could "actual observations" be made of sexual responses in children age two months to fifteen years old?[20] And this is the man whose ideas have been so influential in shaping American sex education.

Wilhelm Reich's life likewise reveals the flaws in his own philosophy. Reich demanded complete sexual freedom for himself and conducted multiple affairs, but he couldn't stand the thought that his wife might live by the same sexual philosophy. His third wife writes that he was desperately jealous and forbade her from living as he did.[21] The test of whether any worldview is true is whether it corresponds to reality. Can we live with it? Obviously Reich could not.

After reading about the personal lives of Sanger, Kinsey, and Reich, and the ideologies they presented, what personal convictions do you now have concerning the role of sex education? _____
_____
_____
_____

The truth is that sexual liberation has been no high road to salvation for those who have worshiped at its shrine. Instead, the tragic results of sexual licentiousness have spread across our entire society, producing an epidemic of abortion, sexually transmitted diseases (afflicting one out of four women), and children born out of wedlock, with all the attendant social pathologies, including school problems, drug and alcohol abuse, and crime. Yet for many Americans, sexual liberation remains a cherished right, and the utopian visions planted by Sanger, Kinsey, Reich, and Calderone continue to flourish. Their ideas still form the unspoken assumptions in the sex education curricula used throughout our public school system.

We all base our lives on some vision of ultimate reality that gives meaning to our individual existence. If we reject God, we will put something in His place; we will absolutize some part of creation. That's exactly what has happened with those who look to a sexual utopia for fulfillment and salvation. Biology takes the place of God as the ultimate reality, and sex becomes the path to the divine.

The irony is that those who reject religion most emphatically, who insist most noisily that they are "scientific," end up promoting what can only be called a religion. In fact, this seems to be a common malady among those who pride themselves on being scientific. Back in the Age of Reason, science was offered as a substitute for religion. But what few foresaw then is that in the process, science itself took on the functions of religion, so that today science is one of the most popular forms of redemption.

Turn to 1 Corinthians 6 and answer the following questions.

Paul writes that the body was meant for whom? _____

What connection do our bodies have with Christ? _____

What sin is not outside our bodies? _____
_____
_____

We all base our lives on some vision of ultimate reality that gives meaning to our individual existence. If we reject God, we will put something in His place; we will absolutize some part of creation. That's exactly what has happened with those who look to a sexual utopia for fulfillment and salvation.

What does Paul refer to our bodies as being?

_____

_____

What should we do with our bodies?

_____

✅ Points to Remember

List two key points of today's session.

1. _____

_____

2. _____

_____

❓ Questions to Ask

What questions do I have concerning what I've read today? _____

_____

_____

_____

🛡 Actions to Take

Based on what I've read, what specific action(s) should I take? _____

_____

_____

_____

_____

✴ Prayers to Pray

Today, God, you taught me _____

_____

_____

_____

_____

_____

Help me, Lord, to _____

_____

_____

_____

_____

[1] Quiz taken from a brochure: Human Development Resource Council, Inc. Norcross, Georgia 30093; copyright 1989; revised 1996. Brochure can be ordered from LIFE CYCLE BOOKS, P.O. Box 420, Lewiston, NY 14092-0420; (800) 214-5849.)

[2] Bernard N. Nathanson, _Why I'm Still Catholic_, ed. Kevin and Marilyn Ryan (New York: Riverhead Books, 1998), 281.

[3] Augustine, _Confessions_ (New York: Penguin, 1961), 151, 170.

[4] Bernard N. Nathanson, _The Hand of God: A Journey from Death to Life by the Abortion Doctor Who Changed His Mind_ [Washington, D.C.: Regnery, 1996], 58-61.

[5] Ibid., 193.

[6] Nathanson, _Why I'm Still Catholic_, 282.

[7] "Pray, Act, Know" is taken from the brochure "Life Light:Focus 2000:The Sanctity of Human Life" published by the Southern Baptist Convention's Ethics & Religious Liberty Commission, 901 Commerce St. #550, Nashville, TN 37203, (615) 244-2495)

[8] James B. Twitchell, _Adcult U.S.A.: The Triumph of Advertising in American Culture_ (New York: Columbia University Press, 1996), 45.

[9] Calvin Coolidge, as quoted in Twitchell, _Adcult U.S.A._, vii.

[10] Mary Midgley, _Evolution as a Religion: Strange Hopes and Stranger Fears_ (New York: Methuen, 1985), 30-35.

[11] Vladimir Lenin, as quoted in Francis Nigel Lee, _Communism versus Creation_ (Nutley, N.J.: Craig Press, 1969), 28.

[12] Klaus Bockmuehl, _The Challenge of Marxism_ (Leicester, England: InterVarsity Press, 1980), 17.

[13] Karl Marx and Frederick Engels, "Private Property and Communism," in _Collected Works_, vol.3 (New York: International Publishers, 1975), 304 (emphasis in the original)..

[14] Margaret Sanger, _The Pivot of Civilization_ (New York: Brentanos, 1922), 232.

[15] Ibid.

[16] Ibid., 233.

[17] Alfred C. Kinsey, _Sexual Behavior in the Human Male_ (Philadelphia: W.B. Saunders, 1948), 59.

[18] Mary S. Calderone and Eric W. Johnson, _The Family Book About Sexuality_ (Harper & Row, 1981), 171.

[19] James H. Jones, "Annals of Sexology," _New Yorker_ (August 25, 1997): 98.

[20] Judith A. Reisman and Edward W. Eichel, _Kinsey, Sex, and Fraud: The Indoctrination of a People_ (Lafayette, La.: Huntington House, 1990), 29-30.

[21] Eustace Chesser, _Salvation through Sex: The Life and Work of Wilhelm Reich_ (New York: William Morrow, 1973), 44.

Who Has the Right Answer?

Is our salvation in the New Age Movement or within the scientific community? In this session, you will look closely at the actions of a loving God to bring us into a relationship with Him.

DAY ONE
Scientific Salvation

"But the Lord said to Samuel, "Do not consider his appearance or his height, for I have rejected him. The Lord does not look at the things man looks at. Man looks at the outward appearance, but the Lord looks at the heart" (1 Samuel 16:7).

When the movie *Independence Day* hit the theaters in the late 1990s, many viewers had the eerie feeling they had seen the story somewhere before.[1] In effect, they had. The film was essentially a remake of the 1954 science-fiction classic *War of the Worlds*—but with one significant difference. In the 1954 movie, the scientists' weapon to kill the invading aliens is destroyed, and the panicking population is forced to turn to God. Churches are jammed with people praying, and their prayers are answered: The aliens contract earthborn bacteria and suddenly die off. "All that men could do had failed," says a final voice-over, and deliverance came from the hand of God alone. The film ends with a scene of people standing on a hillside, singing praise to God.[2]

The contemporary update is quite different—signaling a dramatic change in American culture within only a few decades. *Independence Day* nods politely in God's direction by showing people praying for help. But real deliverance comes through the deployment of advanced military technology: A few strategically placed bombs blow up the aliens and save the world. Indeed, *Independence Day* is a celluloid expression of a widespread belief in science and technology as means of salvation.

Daniel Quinn, author of *Ishmael*, has put his finger squarely on the assumptions that float around in the minds of most Western people, many of whom hold this basic worldview without even realizing that they do. Because the worldview has no name, no label, no church, no rituals, most people don't identify it as a religion or even as a distinctive belief system. It's simply part of the furniture of the Western mind. Yet it is nothing less than a vision of redemption, a surrogate salvation, a substitute for the kingdom of God, setting up science as the path to utopia.

The religion of progress through science really took off after Charles Darwin published his theory of evolution by natural selection. By providing scientific sanction for evolution, Darwin's theory gave enormous impetus to the idea of endless universal progress.[3] English philosopher Herbert Spencer expanded evolution into a comprehensive philosophy covering all of reality—from stars to societies. In his system, the goal of evolutionary progress is the emergence of human beings, who, in turn, will help produce something new and better for the next stage of evolution. Spencer's gospel of evolution became a secular substitute for Christian hope. As religion and physics professor Ian Barbour writes, "Faith in progress replaced the doctrines of creation and providence as assurance that the universe is not really purposeless."[4]

In the 1930s, the great geneticist H. J. Muller divided the history of life into three stages: In the first stage, life was completely at the mercy of the environment; in the second stage, human beings appeared and reversed that order, learning how to reach out and control the environment; and in the dawning third stage, humans would reach inside and control their own nature. Humanity will "shape itself into an increasingly sublime creation—a being beside which the mythical divinities of the past will seem more and more ridiculous," Muller wrote. This godlike being surveys the entire universe, and, "setting its own marvelous inner powers against the brute Goliath of the suns and planets, challenges them to contest."[5]

Muller was an excellent scientist, but what he is describing here is not science. It is science turned into a myth of salvation.

Summarize the contributions Charles Darwin, Herbert Spencer, and H.J. Muller made to promote science as savior.

Darwin:_____

_____

Spencer: _____

_____

Muller: _____

_____

But will such a salvation really save us? How does this vision of redemption stack up in a test against reality? Not very well.

Science itself gives no moral guidelines for our genetic experimentation. How do we decide which traits we want? Do we want to create a Super-Einstein or a Super-Mother Teresa. Do we want to create a class of subhuman slaves to do our menial work? These questions presuppose a standard of values, which science itself cannot provide.

More important, the sheer attempt to remake human nature genetically would strip people of their dignity and reduce them to commodities. With technology offering greater choice and control over the embryo's traits, having a child could become like purchasing a consumer product. And children themselves may come to be regarded as products that we plan, create, modify, improve, and evaluate according to standards of quality control. What happens if the "product" doesn't meet the parents' standard—if they don't think they're getting their money's worth?

Will the child be tossed aside, like an appliance that stops working? As one theologian argues, human beings are "begotten, not made," and if we reverse that—if children become products that we manufacture—their human dignity is lost.[6]

Unfortunately, objections like these are not likely to be raised in a climate where scientists hold a faith in inevitable progress, for the Escalator Myth creates the expectation that change will always be for the better. This explains why scientists reveal a disturbingly uncritical acceptance of genetic engineering. But clearly, change can be either an improvement or a degeneration. New forms of technology can be used in the service of either good or evil. The idea that we can save ourselves through science can be sustained only if we shut our eyes to the human capacity for barbarism.

From what you have read in this book so far and from your knowledge of the Bible, how would you answer the question, "Can a person save himself through science?" _____

_____

_____

Many thoughtful scientists find it hard to go along with such a blind faith. Yet rather than look for another form of salvation, they simply transfer the Escalator Myth to a different galaxy. Because planet Earth is so mired down in pollution, war, and other pathologies, they say, we are likely to destroy ourselves before we manage to evolve to a higher stage.

Carl Sagan built an entire worldview out of his vision of the cosmos as our creator and savior. For him, SETI (Search for Extra-Terrestrial Intelligence) was not just a scientific project; it would be, quite literally, the source of the world's redemption. His reasoning went like this: Any society capable of transmitting messages to us must be far more technologically sophisticated than our own. Therefore, the receipt of a message from space would give us "an invaluable piece of knowledge," telling us "that it is possible to live through [the] technological adolescence" through which we are now passing.[7] No such message has ever been detected.

A familiar hymn to many, "This Is My Father's World," reflects the grandeur of what God has created and our response to Him for His handiwork. Use words from the list below to complete each blank.

This is my Father's world, And to my listening (1) _____, All nature sings and round me (2) _____ The music of the spheres.
This is my Father's world. I rest me in the (3) _____ of rocks and (4) _____ of skies and seas; His hand the wonders wrought.

This is my Father's world, The birds their carols (5) _____, All morning light, the lily (6) _____ Declares their Maker's praise.
This is my Father's world, He shines in all that's (7) _____; In the rustling grass I hear Him (8) _____ He speaks to me everywhere.

This is my Father's world, O let me ne'er (9) _____ That though the wrong seems oft so (10) _____, God is the Ruler yet.
This is my Father's world, The battle is not (11) _____; Jesus who died shall be (12) _____, And earth and heaven be one.

(strong-10; raise-5; ears-1; rings-2; trees-4; thought-3; white-6; fair-7; satisfied-12; pass-8; forget-9; done-11)

(If you know the melody to this song, take a moment now to sing it in your own heart. If not, reread these words in the quiet meditation of your heart.)

So this is where the great promise of science and technology leads us—not to a glorious earthly utopia, but to a fantasy-world escape from this planet and from the horrors that this same technology has created! This view of salvation is no more rational than the demented dreams of the Heaven's Gate cult—thirty-nine intelligent, well-educated people who ingested cocktails of alcohol and drugs in the hope that, by leaving their bodies behind, their spirits would meet up with a comet and move on to the "Level above Human." In their case, the Escalator Myth proved deadly.

History offers no evidence that knowledge will save human society. To the contrary, the problem with Hitler and Stalin was not that they were stupid or ignorant of the laws of cultural evolution; the problem was that they were evil. Bigger and better technology simply gives people bigger and better means to carry out either good or evil choices.

What is the danger of trusting only in technology?_____
_____

Trust in technology is a misguided form of salvation; some things are simply not amenable to a technical quick fix. It is the human heart that determines how we will use our machines—whether we will fashion them into swords or plowshares. Instead of scanning the skies for messages from other galaxies, it is far more realistic to seek the God who made those heavens and who came to reveal the truth by living among us. We don't need radio messages from extraterrestrials; we already have a message from God Himself, and it is found in an ancient Book that proclaimed the creation of the cosmos long before there were astronomers around to muse over such questions. The message begins: "In the beginning God created the heavens and the earth" (Gen. 1:1).

Properly understood, science is a wonderful tool for investigating God's world. But science cannot solve the human dilemma, and it cannot give us hope and meaning. And ultimately, those who exalt science into a religion discover this—which is why they finally give in to a profound pessimism, adrift on a space station called Earth, waiting for a beacon from beyond to save us from ourselves.

But for those less inclined to fantasy, there is no escape from the dreadful realization that a world without God can end only in despair.

Turn in the Old Testament to 1 Samuel 16:1-13 and answer the following questions.
1. What did God instruct Samuel to do?

_____

2. What was Samuel's response to God?

_____

3. What was God's answer to Samuel?

_____

4. When Samuel saw Eliab what did he declare?_____

5. What is the difference between that which man looks upon and that which God looks upon? _____

_____

✅ Points to Remember
List two key points of today's session.
1. _____

_____

2. _____

_____

❓ Questions to Ask
What questions do I have concerning what I've read today? _____

_____

👥 Actions to Take
Based on what I've read, what specific action(s) should I take? _____

_____

_____

✳️ Prayers to Pray
Today, God, you taught me _____

_____

_____

Help me, Lord, to _____

_____

DAY TWO
Worldview of Despair

"I have told you these things, so that in me you may have peace. In this world you will have trouble. But take heart! I have overcome the world" (John 16:33).

For many modern thinkers, the alternative to the Christian message of salvation is not an artificial salvation but a free fall into pessimism and despair. For many people today, there is no transcendent purpose, no expectation of redemption, no answer to life's most wrenching dilemmas, and the courageous person is the one who faces reality squarely and shakes off all illusory hopes.

Identify some people today: (fill-in-the-blank)
For many people today . . .
1. there is no _____ purpose.

2. there is no _____ of redemption.
3. there is no _____ to life's most wrenching dilemmas.
4. The _____ person is the one who faces reality squarely and shakes off all illusory hope.

Yet, ironically, even this pessimism is often held with a fervor that resembles faith. Like the antihero in literature, who is really the hero, this is an antifaith that actually functions as a faith.

What happened to the utopian dreams of the past two centuries, the vision of endless upward progress? They crashed in the convulsions of two world wars that left a trail of horrors, from the blood-soaked trenches of Argonne to the ashes of Auschwitz. From 1918 to 1945, just a little more than a quarter century, the world was shocked out of its complacent optimism by the inescapable reality of naked evil.

European intellectuals who experienced the madness firsthand, on their native soil, were the first to preach a philosophy of despair. "There are no divine judges or controllers," proclaimed French philosopher Jean-Paul Sartre. "The world is all there is, our existence is all we have." Thus was born the word *existentialism*. In his play *No Exit*, one character distills the existentialist creed to a catch phrase: "You are your life, and that's all you are."[8] *There is no higher purpose or goal or meaning to life.*

Albert Camus, another post-World War II existentialist, probed the problem of meaninglessness in *The Myth of Sisyphus*, based on a classical mythology story in which Sisyphus is punished by the gods by being required to push a boulder to the top of a hill, only to have it roll down again. For Camus, this mythological figure represents "the absurd hero," the person who recognizes the absurdity of existence and rebels against it. Since the universe is "without a master," Camus writes, *all that's left for the absurd hero is to exercise his free choice and embrace the absurdity, thereby becoming his own master.*[9]

In the 1960s, Sartre's and Camus' books, which became very popular among American intellectuals and university students, fed into the antiestablishment mood of the Vietnam era. If naturalistic science leads to the conclusion that there is no ultimate meaning to life—life is absurd—then why not seek alternative sources of meaning in sensual pleasure and mind-altering drug experiences?

Summarize the basic beliefs of Sartre and Camus.

Sartre:_____
_____
_____
_____

Camus: _____
_____
_____
_____

Make no mistake. The sixties was not just an era of long hair and bell bottoms. It was an intellectual and cultural upheaval that marked the end of modernity's optimism and that introduced the worldview of despair on a broad level. Ideas concocted in the rarefied domain of academia filtered down to shape an entire generation of young people. They, in turn, have brought those ideas to their logical conclusion in postmodernism, with its wholesale rejection of reason and objective truth.

It is a gloomy picture, but many have found it all the more attractive for its gloom, shuddering "in delicious horror" before it, writes one historian. In fact, starting in the nineteenth century "Many believed it because it was so dreadful; they prided themselves on their courage in facing facts."[10]

How was science creating a gloomy picture?

_____

The creeds of pessimism often take on a distinctly Darwinist cast. Darwin's theory suggests that human beings are merely advanced animals competing in the struggle for existence—that nature is "red in tooth and claw," in the words of Alfred Lord Tennyson. All life forms are driven to compete for the next rung on the evolutionary ladder, leaving the weak behind. This dark side of Darwinism remained an undercurrent, causing few ripples in the reigning myth of progress until recent decades, when it burst forth in what is known as sociobiology—today often called evolutionary psychology (discussed briefly in an earlier session). Sociobiology is an attempt to explain the influence of evolution on human values. In doing so, it tends to take on the functions of religion, for it is impossible to discuss values without stumbling onto the most basic religious questions.

Starting with the Darwinian assumption that those who are most competitive come out on top, sociobiologists conclude that evolution requires ruthlessly selfish behavior. Even actions that appear to be aimed at the benefit of others are grounded in underlying selfishness: We are nice to others only so they will be nice to us. Love and altruism are an illusion, a cover-up for underlying self-interest. In the words of one sociobiologist, there is "no hint of genuine charity" among humans or any other organism. In the cold light of science, as students we turn out to be selfish to the core.

How was Darwinism creating a spirit of pessimism?_____

_____

_____

Now, we might agree that taking care of our own family members has a tinge of self-interest. But what about cooperation and altruism that reaches beyond family or kin? What about the heroic passerby who rescues a drowning child? Even that is reducible to genetic selfishness says science writer Mark Ridley in *The Origins of Virtue.* He argues that any organism intelligent enough to remember individuals and keep tabs will discover that it is sometimes in our interest to help others—because they might someday help us in return. And if it's in our interest, then it will be preserved by natural selection. Even the most selfless behavior can be explained by selfish genes.

In short, sociobiology attributes genes with consciousness, will, and choice while reducing humans to machines that carry out their orders. This is a worldview in which genes become the deity—the ultimate creators and controllers of life.

How do genes become the deity? _____

_____

_____

_____

Even scientists go back and forth, speaking sometimes as if they take the idea of selfish genes literally. "I shall argue that a predominant quality to be expected in a successful gene is ruthless selfishness," writes Dawkins. "Let us try to teach generosity and altruism, because we are born selfish."[11] Notice how he leaps from genes to humans, using the word "selfish" in exactly the same sense, with all its moral connotations. In the "religion of the gene," selfishness is the original sin.

Indeed, sociobiology has all the essential elements of religion. It tells us where we came from: Random chemicals linked up to form the rudimentary DNA, until finally some DNA discovered how to construct bodies for themselves. It tells us what's wrong with us: The fatal flaw in human nature is that we are selfish—a selfishness that reaches far beyond our conscious moral choices and is firmly embedded in our genes. But whereas most worldviews go on to offer a proposal for remedying the basic flaw in human nature, sociobiology offers no remedy. It presents the human being as a puppet in the control of immoral, scheming genes, with no real hope of ever breaking free. It is a religion with no hope of redemption. Life is reduced to perpetual warfare, while the gene is elevated to an evil and destructive demon, driven to overcome all competitors in the struggle for existence.

Thus, sociobiology can be understood as a contemporary form of those fatalistic religions that tap into the human fascination with power and destruction. In sociobiology the "deity being worshiped is power," writes British philosopher Mary Midgley. Adherents "offer us a mystique of power" located in the genes.[12]

In your opinion, what could possibly make such a negative faith appealing? _____

_____

_____

It offers one compensation: It gives adherents a way to debunk conventional religion and morality. It dispels the "illusion" that there is a loving, sovereign God and that human beings have dignity and significance as genuine moral agents. Atheism is presented as the conclusion when it is, in fact, the hidden premise.

And if your premise is rejection of the biblical God, then no matter how sophisticated your theories, you will end in despair. For these pessimistic myths are right about one thing: A universe without God is indeed purposeless, meaningless, and impersonal.

Imagine yourself writing a note to a friend on campus who has been discouraged by life's events. What would you say to encourage her to seek God for a meaningful, personal relationship? _____

_____

_____

_____

A full-page ad for Schwinn bicycles shows a young man leaping high into the air on his Schwinn; at the bottom of the page is a picture of a coffin being lowered into the ground with ad copy that taunts the reader: "What, a little death frightens you?" Schwinn is clearly marketing more than bikes; it is telling kids that it is cool to court death.

Since when did playing with death become chic? Since a pervasive sense of meaningless has left many people so jaded that it takes a whiff of danger to restore a sense of ultimacy. And what is more intense, more ultimate, than coming face-to-face with death?

What do you believe makes some people flirt with death? _____

_____

_____

This mind-set may explain the growing popularity of high-risk sports, from hang gliding to rock climbing to street luge to sky diving. When *U.S. News and World Report* ran a cover story on the topic of high-risk sports, one subhead read: "The peril, the thrill, the sheer rebellion of it all."[13] Like Camus' absurd hero, this is rebellion against the absurdity, against the futility of life, where everything we love or live for ends in death. In a society reduced to sterile secularism, the only response left is to look death squarely in the face and spit on it. This is the ultimate, heroic existentialist response.

On June 19, 1998, NBC ran an extensive news feature that interviewed people who had signed on to chase tornadoes. What's the attraction? The excitement of a brush with death. One man said coming close to a tornado was "a religious experience."[14]

This is all that's left for a culture that has plumbed the depths of absurdity: daredevil antics in the face of death. And when the antics grow old, there is only death itself.

Hidden Word Search
Circle the eleven hidden words which could describe a person in despair. As you're looking for these words, also locate the Person who gives us peace.

```
M S I M I S S E P I M P E R S O N A L S
O S S E L E S O P R U P I S A U N D I U
M E A N I N G L E S S E N I L E N O L S
D E T A E F E D U P O I N T L E S S P E
H O P E L E S S E V I T C U R T S E D J
```

(pessimism, impersonal, loneliness, destructive,
hopeless, meaningless, pointless, purposeless,
defeated, Jesus)

In the end, those who deny the God of the Bible and history have only two choices: they can either trivialize death by defying it or control death by embracing it on their own terms. We have played out the logical consequences of the Enlightenment's rejection of God and brought us to complete despair of any transcendent truth or meaning. The blazing, optimistic hope that humanity is moving ever upward and onward, boldly progressing to a new stage in evolution, has been replaced by bitter cynicism. Marooned on the rocks of reality, science itself now promises only the near-comical fantasy that we might be rescued by extraterrestrials from outer space.

What two choices do people have when they deny God?

1. _____
_____

2. _____
_____

One might think that upon hitting the dead end of despair, men and women would be driven to return to the Creator. But, alas, although it is true that "our hearts find no peace until they rest in [God]," the human instinct is to flee Him.[15] For finding God will cost us our cherished autonomy.

Turn to John 16:17-33 and answer the following questions.

1. **What analogy is Jesus making in comparing His disciples with a woman giving birth?**
_____
_____
_____

2. **The Christian's joy depends on what?**
_____
_____

3. **What does asking in Jesus' name mean for the believer?** _____
_____
_____
_____

4. **Why can you as a Christian student be at peace?** _____
_____
_____
_____

✔ Points to Remember
List two key points of today's session.
1. _____
_____
2. _____
_____

❓ Questions to Ask
What questions do I have concerning what I've read today? _____
_____
_____
_____

✇ Actions to Take
Based on what I've read, what specific action(s) should I take? _____
_____
_____
_____

✶ Prayers to Pray
Today, God, you taught me _____
_____
_____
_____
_____

Help me, Lord, to _____
_____
_____

Seeking the Divine in the New Age Movement

"The Lord is not slow in keeping his promise, as some understand slowness. He is patient with you, not wanting anyone to perish, but everyone to come to repentance" (2 Peter 3:9).

When the bright image of science and progress began to fade and when optimism gave way to disillusionment and despair, many people began to cast about for new answers. Asian religions, especially Hinduism and Buddhism, have always enchanted people from Western cultures to some degree, and now these religions have become popular alternatives to the dominant Western worldview.

And the attraction is powerful. Western secularism is materialistic, limiting reality to what can be tested scientifically. Eastern mysticism is spiritual, opening the consciousness to new levels of awareness. Western thought is analytical, leading to fragmentation and alienation. Eastern thought is holistic, promising healing and wholeness. Western science has destroyed the environment and polluted the air. Eastern pantheism proffers a new respect for nature.

Jot down two or three thoughts you have about the New Age movement.

1. _____
   _____
2. _____
   _____
3. _____
   _____
   _____

In the 1960s, many young people turned to Eastern religion to fill their spiritual emptiness, giving rise to the New Age movement. Today the movement has become so mainstream that community colleges offer classes in yoga, tai chi, astrology, and therapeutic touch. The New Age movement is also a major commercial success. Free copies of slick New Age community resources publications are available at the local supermarket, advertising everything from holistic health practices to past-life therapy.

Actor Richard Gere is devout. In 1984, he converted to Tibetan Buddhism and now spends several months each year traveling and speaking on behalf of the Dali Lama. Then there is Steven Segal, who has been recognized by the supreme head of the Tibetan-based Nyingma lineage as a *tulku* (a reincarnated lama), as well as a *terton* (a revealer of truth). Think of that the next time you watch Segal on film breaking an enemy's neck.

What are two ways we have been influenced by the New Age movement?

1. _____
2. _____

It may seem that the New Age movement appeared out of nowhere in the 1960s, but the way had been prepared in the Romantic movement of the nineteenth century, which was itself a kind of counterculture in its day. As we saw in the last session, sensitive people could already see that science was creating a picture of the world as a vast machine, inexorably grinding its gears, with no place for beauty or meaning or purpose. So the Romantics cast about for an alternative, just as the children of the sixties did, and they revived an ancient philosophy known as neo-Platonism, a blend of Greek thought and Eastern mysticism. They tossed out the metaphor of the universe as a machine and replaced it with the metaphor of the universe as an organism, a living thing, animated by a "Life Force."

Everything is alive, the Romantics said. Even matter itself, they thought, has a rudimentary form of life or consciousness. And what is the major characteristic of life? Growth. Development. Just as each organism unfolds in stages according to an inner law of development, so life itself unfolds in definite stages from simple to complex under the direction of the Life Force.

What we see is that for a long time, in the arts, philosophy, and even theology, the Western world has been embracing ideas compatible with Eastern pantheism. All it took was a widespread disillusionment with Western culture to send these ideas hurtling into the mainstream.

In what ways has the Romantic movement influenced the New Age movement? _____

_____

_____

_____

Today, New Age thinking pervades Western society, spawning a host of techniques used in medicine, business, education, the military, and even—tragically—churches. Various meditation exercises are sold as means for resolving conflict and for enhancing relaxation, creativity, self-esteem, and even physical health. For exam-

ple, at Stanford University's Graduate School of Business, a seminar on "Creativity in Business" includes meditation, chanting, "dream work," tarot cards, and a discussion of the "New Age Capitalist."[16] Government agencies as well as private businesses spend millions of dollars in contracts with consulting companies that use New Age techniques for management training.

Education is only one avenue for New Age ideas. They turn up in every outlet of popular culture. Books about the New Age, for example, enjoy a commanding position on bookstore shelves, often crowding out traditional religious works. If you opened a book and read, "I looked and saw a new heaven and a new earth," you might think you were reading the book of Revelation in the Bible. Instead, it is the opening of James Redfield's megahit *The Tenth Insight*. The words are indeed from Revelation, but that's the closest link to anything biblical.

What are two areas in which the New Age movement has had an influence?

1. _____

2. _____

Clearly, the New Age movement should not be laughed off as a silly fad. It is the vehicle for a complete worldview, offering an answer to all three major life questions.

Answer each question with one of the New Age responses below:

1. Where did we come from and who are we?

_____

_____

2. What has gone wrong with the world?

_____

_____

3. What is the source of our salvation?

_____

_____

Responses:

1. We must rediscover our true nature and link up to the God within.

2. We are somehow fragmented off from the Universal Spirit.
3. We have forgotten our true nature, forgotten that we are part of God.

Like all forms of the Escalator Myth, this one starts with utopian premises. There is no real evil, only ignorance: We have forgotten who we are. And by the same token, there is no real redemption, only enlightenment: We must recover a mystical knowledge of our inner divinity. This we do by various techniques, such as meditation, relaxation and breathing exercises, guided imagery, visualization, and use of crystals, all aimed at producing a state of consciousness in which the boundaries of the self dissolve and we gain a sense of unity with the divine. Through this higher consciousness, a person is said to tap into divine power and become more creative, more energetic, and even capable of healing illnesses through the power of the mind.

But like all forms of utopianism, this offer of salvation is hollow. By denying the reality of sin, it fails to address the crucial truth of our existence—that we are fallen creatures prone to evil. Proponents of the New Age reassure us that alienation and strife exist only on the superficial level of existence; at the deepest level, we are one with each other in God. As we become aware of this unity, they assert, we will begin to treat each other with kindness and charity.

Write a characteristic of Christianity and the New Age movement below each of the following concepts:

EVIL:
Christianity-_____
_____
New Age Movement-_____
_____

REDEMPTION:
Christianity-_____
_____

New Age Movement-_____
_____

SALVATION:
Christianity-_____
_____
New Age Movement-_____
_____

SIN:
Christianity-_____
_____
New Age Movement-_____
_____

However, this view of human nature simply doesn't stack up against reality. Mere knowledge is not enough to undercut the evil in the human heart. Simply knowing what is right doesn't enable us to do right. This is the dilemma the apostle Paul wrestled with: The good that I want to do, I don't do (see especially in the New Testament in the book of Romans 7:14-25). We don't need to have our consciousness raised; we need to be saved.

The New Age god cannot save us. It is an impersonal spiritual substratum of energy underlying all things. He—or rather, it—is more akin to electricity than to a deity. It is a power people try to plug into, not a personal God whom people can love and with whom they can communicate.

Why can the New Age movement not save us?_____
_____
_____

Moreover, for all its promises about raising self-esteem, the New Age gospel does nothing to affirm the worth of the individual; it offers no basis for human dignity and meaning. On the contrary, the goal of all meditation techniques is to lose the individual self, to dissolve it in the Universal Spirit, just as a drop of water dissolves in the ocean. How utterly unlike the biblical

God, who created us as individuals, who watches over each of us, who has numbered "even the very hairs of your head" (Matt. 10:30).

Furthermore, New Age philosophy gives us no basis for morality. If God is in everything, God is in both good and evil; therefore, there is no final difference between them. Morality is only a method for purifying the soul from desires so that it can attain mystical consciousness, like the eightfold path of Buddhism.[17]

How does New Age not give us a basis for morality? _____

_____

_____

But the ultimate failure of New Age thinking is its sheer implausibility. How many of us are capable of insisting, with a straight face, that we are perfect? Yet New Age proponents actually claim that "we are perfect exactly the way we are. And when we accept that, life works."[18] People who can swallow that have to be deliberately oblivious to their own failures, shortcomings, and sins.

What does New Age say about us being perfect? _____

_____

What lie is recorded in Genesis 3:4-5?

_____

_____

In short, spiritual evolutionism is not merely an error, a mistaken idea; it is religious rebellion against reality—against the sheer fact that God is the Creator and we are creatures. It is the empty boast of the pot that claims to make itself without the need of a Potter.

And today it is making inroads even into Christian institutions. Some mainstream churches hold Gaia conferences dedicated to goddess worship. Sincere Christians read writers like M. Scott Peck, who merges New Age concepts into historic Christian truth. Celebrated clergy like Matthew Fox claim to be Christians even as they promote pagan earth worship.

The danger is that more and more Christians regard religion as therapy. As a college student, you may lower your defenses against worldviews that appeal primarily to our emotions and that demand nothing. The New Age is the perfect religious match for a culture driven by a therapeutic mind-set, hungry to fill the nothingness. It allows its followers to draw on ancient wisdom but to reshape it to fit the fashion of the moment.

By contrast, Christianity makes stringent moral demands on its followers. Critics often dismiss Christianity as mere wish fulfillment, a comforting illusion dreamed up by the ancients. But this characterization is patently foolish. Who, after all, would invent a religion that commands us to give up our lives for one another, to overcome evil with good, to love our enemies, to turn the other cheek, to give our possessions to the poor, to be just and merciful? *Would anyone really design a religion devoted to an all-powerful, sovereign, omniscient God who demands righteousness and submission? A God who dispenses severe judgment?*

No. When as a college student you create your own religion, you create gods and goddesses in your own image. The ancient gods of mythology had limited powers, were subject to human interference, and displayed all the human weaknesses and vices. And the New Age god who is little more than a warm feeling within, or at worst a dabbling in occult powers, is merely a ratification of whatever the human ego wants.

In what ways does Christianity contradict New Age? _____

_____

_____

_____

In the final analysis, any religious worldview must pass the most crucial test: Can it make sense of the human predicament? Does it provide a true source of redemption? Is it true? Applying this test to the New Age worldview, we detect its fatal weaknesses. It fails to correspond to reality as we experience it.

And if there is no answer in the West and no answer in the East, where does one turn?

Turn to 2 Peter 3:1-13 and answer the following questions.

What does Peter say will happen "in the last days"? _____

_____

When people are too proud and corrupt, what do they forget? _____

_____

Why is God referred to as being "patient"?

_____

What kind of people does Peter challenge his readers to be? _____

_____

Points to Remember
List two key points of today's session.

1. _____

_____

2. _____

_____

Questions to Ask
What questions do I have concerning what I've read today? _____

_____

_____

Actions to Take
Based on what I've read, what specific action(s) should I take? _____

_____

_____

Prayers to Pray
Today, God, you taught me _____

_____

_____

_____

Help me, Lord, to _____

_____

_____

_____

DAY FOUR
Searching for Salvation

"Therefore, if anyone is in Christ, he is a new creation; the old has gone, the new has come!" (2 Corinthians 5:17).

Everywhere Americans turn, we are bombarded with different options clamoring for our allegiance. The merchants in the marketplace of ideas hock their wares. Believe this, and find peace of mind! Believe that, and be more successful in life! Join this group, follow that method, and achieve your most cherished goals. Whether the trappings are secular or religious, all the offers, in essence, attempt to answer the questions all people and all ages have asked: *What gives our lives meaning and purpose? Is there a way out of the human predicament of suffering and evil? Where is our hope and salvation?*

Today's most fashionable answers presume that there is no kingdom of God, and therefore they promise to create one here on earth. As we have seen, they fail to deliver on this promise. Commercialism boldly utilizes a religious appeal to entice us to buy more products. Neo-Marxism has won over nearly a generation of students and activists with a single basic format: Cast off the oppressors, and the utopian society of equality will emerge. For many Americans, the siren call of the gospel of sex is appealing. But perhaps the West's most powerful idols have been science and technology with their myth of progress.

The glaring inadequacy of all these proffers of salvation has led many people to embrace exotic religious movements from the East. But Eastern methods of spirituality propose to dissolve the individual in the Cosmic Spirit, thus failing to answer the cry of the individual heart for meaning and spiritual significance.

By lining up the Christian faith against other worldviews and religions, as we have done in the previous sessions, we see with astonishing clarity that Christianity offers the only real answers to the most basic questions of life and the best understanding of how we can be saved.

First, Christianity begins with an accurate diagnosis of the problem, of the human dilemma. God created us and established the moral dimensions for our lives. But we blew it. We have sinned, every one of us; we have all fallen short of God's perfect standard.

Read Romans 3:23 and rewrite this verse in your own words. _____
_____

We have defied the moral order of the universe, and, as a result, we are alienated from God.

Admittedly, people often do not feel guilty before God, since we are indoctrinated with the belief that guilt is merely a subjective feeling, a neurosis to be cured, and that we really ought to feel good about ourselves. As a result, many people come to Christianity on grounds other than guilt: a longing for inner peace, an attraction to the quality of love practiced in a local church, or a need to resolve some life crisis. But no matter what initially attracts us to Christianity, at some point each of us must confront the truth of our own moral condition: Guilt is objectively real, and we are guilty. We are sinners in the hands of a righteous God. The Holy Spirit can penetrate the hardest heart to convict us of our sinfulness. I know, because that is exactly what the Spirit did in my life.

What testimony can you share concerning the Holy Spirit convicting you of your sinfulness?
_____
_____
_____

Second, just as Christianity gives an accurate diagnosis of the problem, it also provides the only answer. God Himself reaches across the moral chasm that separates us from Him, and He brings us back. In His great love for His creation, God devised a way that He could pay the punishment; He satisfied the demands of divine justice, yet He spared us. God Himself became a man, lived a perfect life in obedience to the moral order, and in His death suffered the blow of divine justice and paid the penalty we rightly deserve for our sins. With that substitutionary atonement, God can justify the sinner and yet remain just—to be both "just and the one who justifies".

Read Romans 3:26 and rewrite this verse in your own words. _____
_____
_____

God can forgive sin without turning a blind eye to the moral law that flows from

His own holy character. God's righteousness is vindicated, and yet He can also bestow mercy on those who call on Him.

What does the Bible say about our response to salvation? Read the following Scriptures and draw a line to the appropriate response.

Acts 2:41   Repentance
Acts 16:31   Belief or trust in God
Philippians 2:11   Reverential awe
                    and respect for God
Matthew 9:8   Knowledge of God
Romans 1:28   Acceptance of God
Matthew 22:37   Love of God
Romans 12:1-2   Obedience to God
Mark 1:15   Confession

We can all be excited about accepting God's salvation. It is available to us all who, by faith, ask the Lord to forgive us our sin and come take up permanent residence in our hearts. Have you called on the Lord for His saving grace? You can do it now!

The death of the God-man is not the end of the story, for Jesus was resurrected from the dead. He overcame death (the effect of sin), making it possible for us to be free from sin and death, from evil and destruction. By receiving His salvation, we become new men and women—a restored creation.

In your own words, how has each of these worldview responses failed to give people real hope and peace?

Politics: _____
_____
_____
_____
_____

Sex: _____
_____
_____
_____
_____
_____

Science: _____
_____
_____
_____
_____
_____

Eastern spirituality: _____
_____
_____
_____
_____
_____
_____

The third and final element that sets Christianity's offer of salvation apart from all other religions and worldviews is its historicity. Christianity is not based on some evolutionary projection millions of years into the future or on some extraterrestrial fantasy. It is based on an historical event at a specific time and place: the crucifixion of Christ during the Jewish Passover in Jerusalem in the year 33 A.D and His resurrection three days later.

What two historical events offer hope for Christians?
1. _____
2. _____

Over the two thousand years since Christ's resurrection, the historical validity of this event has withstood every imaginable assault, ranging from the charge of "a cover-up" (by religious leaders of Jesus' day) to modern claims that it was a "Passover plot" or a "conjuring trick with bones." What skeptics overlook is that the empty tomb was an empirical fact, verified by a number of people, including the soldiers who guarded the tomb (Why else did they need to concoct an alternative explanation?). The resurrected Christ also appeared to five hundred eyewitnesses—too many to explain away as mass hysteria or the power of suggestion.

Read 1 Corinthians 15:3-7 and state the evidence of the risen Christ. _____
_____
_____
_____
_____

Another common stance, especially among theological liberals, is that the historicity of Jesus' death doesn't matter. Even if the events didn't happen, Jesus is an important moral teacher, and the death and resurrection are interesting religious symbols. Mahatma Gandhi expressed this same attitude: "I may say that I have never been interested in an historical Jesus. I should not care if it was proved by someone that the man called Jesus never lived, and that what was narrated in the Gospels was a figment of the writer's imagination. For the Sermon on the Mount would still be true for me."[19]

Why should historical truth matter to college students on your campus? _____
_____
_____
_____
_____
_____
_____

But historical truth does matter. It is not enough to see Jesus' life and death as a symbol, a parable, a myth, a purely subjective idea that can be "true for me," even if others do not believe it. The Christian message is the good news about what God has actually done. But if the gospel is a myth, then God has not done anything. "If religion be made independent of history, there is no such thing as a gospel," wrote the great Christian scholar J. Gresham Machen. "For 'gospel' means 'good news,' tidings, information about something that has happened. A gospel independent of history is a contradiction in terms."[20]

Turn to 2 Corinthians 5:11-21 and answer the following questions.

1. What does Paul say compels us? _____
_____
_____

2. Love for lost people constrains us to do what? _____
_____

3. What does Paul say we are when we are "in Christ"? _____

4. As believers, what ministry has God given us? _____
_____
_____

5. How did we become "the righteousness of God"? _____
_____

✅ Points to Remember
List two key points of today's session.
1. _____
_____
2. _____
_____

❓ Questions to Ask
What questions do I have concerning what I've read today? _____
_____
_____

🛡 Actions to Take
Based on what I've read, what specific action(s) should I take? _____
_____
_____
_____

✳ Prayers to Pray
Today, God, you taught me _____
_____
_____

Help me, Lord, to _____
_____

Who Has the Right Answer?

DAY FIVE

The Validity of Christ

"He redeemed us in order that the blessing given to Abraham might come to the Gentiles through Christ Jesus, so that by faith we might receive the promise of the Spirit" (Galations 3:14).

Jesus' resurrection is much more than an historical fact, but it is nothing less than one. Historical scholarship supports the gospel's claims. Critics used to argue that the New Testament wasn't written until hundreds of years after Jesus lived, by which time a jungle of myth and legend had grown up around the original events. But we now know that most of the New Testament books were written within twenty to forty years after Christ's resurrection. In fact, a few years ago, scholars discovered fragments of a copy of Matthew's Gospel, and the fragments were dated about 50 A.D.—only seventeen years after Jesus' death and resurrection. That means the original Gospel of Matthew had to be written even earlier—within a few years of the events recorded, at a time when many people who knew Jesus were still alive and could dispute any false claims.

Today, Jesus' life is more thoroughly validated than is the life of virtually any other ancient figure. Of the New Testament record alone, we have several thousand copies that date from only a few years after Jesus lived on earth. By contrast, we have only twenty copies of the works of the Roman writer Tacitus, and the earliest manuscript is dated a thousand years after he lived. The earliest manuscript we have of the work of Aristotle is dated fourteen hundred years after he lived. The earliest copy of Caesar's *Gallic Wars* is dated a thousand years after he wrote it. Yet no one questions either the historicity of Tacitus or Aristotle or Caesar, or the authenticity of their writings.

The salvation attested to in the New Testament is the culmination of a long process of preparation in the Old Testament, which is also historical, as archeological discoveries continue to verify. For example, there was a time when critics said Moses could not have written the Pentateuch because writing had not yet been invented. Then archaeologists discovered that writing was well developed thousands of years before Moses' day. Egypt and Babylonia were highly literate cultures, with dictionaries, schools, and libraries.

The discovery of the Dead Sea scrolls has vindicated much of the Old Testament—even its supernatural character. Take Psalm 22, which predicts Christ's crucifixion in uncanny detail. Skeptics, rejecting the reality of divinely inspired prophecy, insisted that it must have been written in the Maccabean Era, just before the birth of Christ, since before then the practice of crucifixion did not exist in the Roman Empire. But when the Dead Sea scrolls were discovered, they included copies of the Psalms dated centuries before the Maccabean Era.

And the evidence continues to mount. In the 1970s, archeological excavations confirmed the unique design of Philistine temples, with the roof supported by two central pillars about six feet apart. This gives historical plausibility to the story of Samson, who grasped two pillars in the Philistine temple and brought it down.

The stories in the Old and New Testaments are not made-up fables; they are accounts of real people and real events in history. As British journalist and historian Paul Johnson concludes, "It is not now the men of faith, it is the skeptics, who have reason to fear the course of discovery."[21]

The old pagan world was littered with myths about a dying god who rises again, writes C. S. Lewis, but in Christianity, the myth became fact. "The dying god really appears—as a historical Person, living in a definite place and time."[22] Like myth, the gospel is a colorful story that inspires our imagination, but it is far more than myth; it is sober fact, something that happened in the real world. The story of Jesus is, Lewis concludes, "Perfect Myth and Perfect Fact: claiming not only our love and our obedience, but also our wonder and delight, addressed to the savage, the child, and the poet in each one of us no less than to the moralist, the scholar and the philosopher."[23]

What did C.S. Lewis mean by "Perfect Myth and Perfect Fact"? _____
_____
_____
_____

But Christianity did not end with the historical record of Christ's resurrection. For at Pentecost, the risen Christ sent forth the Holy Spirit into the lives of believers, to work out His purposes in their lives. Today as well, every believer receives the power to become a child of God, to be transformed and restored to our true nature, people created in the image of God. And we live as the community of hope, in eschatological expectation, knowing that Christ will return and establish His rule over all.

Turn in the New Testament to Acts 2 and read about the day of Pentecost. After reading this account, identify three key points from Peter's message to the crowds (vs. 14-41).

"Peter Addresses the Crowd"

1. _____
   _____
2. _____
   _____
3. _____
   _____

God's redemption, then, does not change us into something different so much as it *restores* in us the image of God, the image that was broken at the Fall. Virtually all of the words describing salvation in the Bible imply a return to something that originally existed. To *redeem* means to "buy back," and the image evokes a kidnapping: Someone has been seized and is being held for ransom; a second person pays the ransom and buys the captive back, restoring the person to original freedom. *Reconciliation* implies a relationship torn by conflict, then returned to its original friendship. The New Testament also speaks of renewal, implying that something has been battered and torn, then restored to its pristine condition. *Regeneration* implies something returned to life after having died. "All these terms suggest a *restoration* of some good thing that was spoiled or lost."[24]

Being justified before God is a wonderful gift, yet it is just the beginning. Salvation empowers us to take up the task laid on the first human beings at the dawn of creation: to subdue the earth and extend the Creator's dominion over all of life.

Only Christianity provides true redemption—a restoration to our created state and the hope of eternal peace with God. No other worldview identifies the real problem: the stain of sin in our souls. Hence, human experience proves that every other means of salvation is false.

Only Christianity liberates us from the ruins of our lives. And having been liberated from sin, only Christianity empowers us to help bring Christ's restoration to the entire creation order.

Turn to Galatians 3:1-14 and answer the following questions.

1. How did Paul say Christians receive the Spirit? _____
_____
_____
_____

2. Who are the children of Abraham? _____
_____
_____
_____

3. How will the righteous live? _____
_____
_____
_____

4. Why did Christ redeem us? _____
_____
_____
_____

✅ Points to Remember

List two key points of today's session.

1. _____
_____

2. _____
_____

❓ Questions to Ask

What questions do I have concerning what I've read today? _____
_____
_____
_____

👥 Actions to Take

Based on what I've read, what specific action(s) should I take? _____
_____
_____

✳️ Prayers to Pray

Today, God, you taught me _____
_____

_____
_____
_____
_____

Help me, Lord, to _____
_____
_____
_____
_____

[1] *Independence Day*, Twentieth Century Fox (1996).

[2] *War of the Worlds*, Paramount Pictures (1953).

[3] Mary Midgley, *Evolution as a Religion: Strange Hopes and Stranger Fears* (New York: Nethien and Co., 1985), 34.

[4] Ian Barbour, *Issues in Science and Religion* (New York: Harper Torchbooks, 1966), 94.

[5] H.J. Muller, as quoted in Mary Midgley, *Evolution as a Religion*, 34.

[6] Oliver O'Donovan, *Begotten or Made?* (London: Oxford University Press, 1984).

[7] Carl Sagan, *Broca's Brain* (New York: Random, 1979), 276.

[8] Jean-Paul Sartre, *No Exit and Three Other Plays* (New York: Random, 1949).

[9] Albert Camus, *The Myth of Sisyphus and Other Essays* (New York: Alfred A. Knopf, 1955).

[10] Randall, *The Making of the Modern Mind*, 581-82

[11] Richard Dawkins, *The Selfish Gene* (London: Oxford University Press, 1976), 2-3.

[12] Midgley, *Evolution as a Religion: Strange Hopes and Stranger Fears*, 131, 140.

[13] Brendan I. Koerner, "Extreeeme," *U.S. News and World Report* (June 30, 1997): 50.

[14] "NBC Nightly News" (June 19, 1998).

[15] Saint Augustine, *Confessions*, book 1, paragraph 1, trans. R.S. Pine-Coffin (New York: Penguin, 1961), 21.

[16] Robert Lindsey, "Spiritual Concepts Drawing a Different Breed of Adherent," *New York Times*, 29 September 1986.

[17] Peter Kreeft, *Fundamentals of the Faith: Essays in Christian Apologetics* (San Francisco: Ignatius Press, 1988), 90.

[18] *Spiritual Counterfeit Project Newsletter* 10 (winter 1984-85).

[19] Mahatma Gandhi, "Address on Christmas Day, 1931," as quoted in A.R. Vidler, *Objections to Christian Belief* (London: Constable, 1963), 59.

[20] J. Gresham Machen, *Christianity and Liberalism* (New York: Macmillan, 1923), 121.

[21] Paul Johnson, "A Historian Looks at Jesus," (a speech first presented at Dallas Theological Seminary in 1986), Sources, no. 1 (1991).

[22] C.S. Lewis, *God in the Dock: Essays on Theology and Ethics* (Grand Rapids: Eerdmans, 1970), 58.

[23] Ibid., 67.

[24] Al Wolters, *Creation Regained: Biblical Basics for a Reformational Worldview* (Grand Rapids: Eerdmans, 1985), 58 (emphasis in the original).

Changing Our Culture

*When the biblical worldview is adopted, your perpective
is changed on how life is to be lived. In this session,
you will look closely at what the world can be like when
college students/young adults perceive
How Now Shall We Live.*

Restoring the Created Order

"For by him all things were created: things in heaven and on earth, visible and invisible, whether thrones or powers or rulers or authorities; all things were created by him and for him" (Colossians 1:16).

The scriptural justification for culture building starts with Genesis. At the dawn of creation, the earth is unformed, empty, dark, and undeveloped. Then, in a series of steps, God establishes the basic creational distinctives: light and dark, "above the expanse" and "below the expanse," sea and land, and so on.

Until the sixth day, God does the creating directly, but after that He changes His strategy. On the sixth day, God creates an image of Himself, the first human beings, and He orders them to carry on where He leaves off: to live in His image and to have dominion.

What two statements does God make in Genesis 1:26?

1. _____
_____
2. _____
_____

Creation is "very good," just as God proclaimed, but the task of exploring and developing its powers and potentialities, the task of building a civilization, God turns over to His image bearers.

It is our contention in this book that the Lord's cultural commission is inseparable from the Great Commission. When we turn to the New Testament, we do not find it specifically commanding believers to be engaged in political issues or the law or education or the arts, but it doesn't need to, because the cultural mandate given to Adam still applies. Every part of creation came from God's hand, every part was drawn into the mutiny of the human race and its enmity toward God, and every part will someday be redeemed. This is the apostle Paul's message to the Romans, in which he promises that "creation itself will be liberated from its bondage to sin and decay" (Rom. 8:21). Redemption is not just for individuals; it is for all God's creation.

Paul makes the point most strongly in Colossians 1:15-20, where he describes the lordship of Christ in three ways: (1) everything was made by and for Christ: "For by him all things were created: things in heaven and on earth, visible and invisible . . . all things were created by him and for him"; (2) everything holds together in Christ: "He is before all things, and in him all things hold together"; (3) everything will be reconciled by Christ: "For God was pleased to have all his fullness dwell in him, and through him to reconcile to himself all things, whether things on earth or things in heaven." Redemption covers all aspects of creation, and the end of time will not signal an end to creation but the beginning of a new heaven and a new earth: God will make all things new (Rev. 21:5).

What two points does Paul make clear in Colossians 1:15-20?

1. _____
_____
2. _____
_____

The lesson is clear: Christians are saved not only *from* something (sin) but also *to* something (Christ's lordship over all of life). The Christian life begins with spiritual restoration through prayer, worship, and exercise of spiritual gifts within a local church. This is the indispensable beginning, for only the redeemed person is filled with God's Spirit and can genuinely know and fulfill God's plan. But then we are meant to proceed to the restoration of all God's creation, which includes private and public virtue; individual and family life; education and community; work, politics, and law; science and medicine; literature, art, and music. This redemptive goal permeates everything we do, for there is no invisible dividing line between sacred and secular. We are to bring "all things" under the lordship of Christ, in the home and the school, in the workshop and the corporate boardroom, on the movie screen and the concert stage, in the city council and the legislative chamber.

Christians are saved not only _____ something ( ) but also _____ something (_____).

This is what we mean when we say a collegiate Christian must have a comprehensive worldview: a view or perspective that covers all aspects of the world. For every aspect of the world was created with a structure, a character, a norm. These underlying principles are God's "laws"—God's design and purpose—for creation and can be known through both special revelation (God's Word given in Scripture) and general revelation (the structure of the world He made). They include both laws of nature and norms for human life.

What does it mean for a collegiate Christian to have a comprehensive worldview? _____
_____
_____
_____

This point must be pressed. We tend to be confident about God's laws for nature, such as gravity, motion, heredity; but we seem far less confident about God's laws for the family, for education, or for the state. Yet a truly Christian worldview draws no such distinction. It insists that God's law governs all creation. And just as we have to learn to live in accord with the law of gravity, so too we must learn to live in accord with God's norms for society.

These two types of laws seem quite different—perhaps because only the latter is, in a sense "voluntary." Stones fall, planets move in their orbits, seasons come and go, and the electron circles the nucleus—all without any choice in the matter—because God rules directly in the physical world. But in culture and society, God rules indirectly, entrusting human beings with the task of making tools, doing justice, producing art and music, educating children, and building houses. And though a stone cannot defy God's law of gravity, college students can rebel against God's created order—and they often do so. Yet that should not blind us to the fact that there is a single objective, universal order covering both nature and human nature.

John's Gospel borrows the Greek word for this universal plan of creation (*logos*) and, in a startling move, identifies it with a personal being—Jesus Christ Himself. "In the beginning was the Word [*Logos*]," which is the source of creation (John 1:1). "Through him all things were made; without him nothing was made that has been made" (John 1:3). In other words, Jesus Himself is the source of the plan or design of creation.

As a result, obedience to Christ means living in accord with that plan in all aspects of life. Friends and church, business and commerce, art and education, politics and law are institutions grounded in God's created order and are not, therefore, arbitrary in their configuration. A school is not a business and shouldn't be run like one;

The lesson is clear: Christians are saved not only from something (sin) but also to something (Christ's lordship over all of life). The Christian life begins with spiritual restoration through prayer, worship, and exercise of spiritual gifts within a local church.

And just as we have to learn to live in accord with the law of gravity, so too we must learn to live in accord with God's norms for society.

Our task is to reclaim that entire created order for His dominion. The world is a spiritual battleground, with two powers contending for the same territory.

In a nutshell, if we reject the biblical teaching about creation, we end up with nature as our creator. Morality then becomes something humans invent when they have evolved to a certain level.

friends are not a state and shouldn't be run like one. Each has its own normative structure, ordained by God, and each has its own sphere of authority under God.[1]

For the Christian, there must be no dichotomy between the sacred and the secular because nothing lies outside of God's created order. Our task is to reclaim that entire created order for His dominion. The world is a spiritual battleground, with two powers contending for the same territory. God's adversary, Satan, has invaded creation and now attempts to hold it as occupied territory. With the death and resurrection of Jesus Christ, God launched a counteroffensive to reclaim His rightful domain, and we are God's soldiers in this ongoing battle. We have been rescued "from the dominion of darkness and brought . . . into the kingdom of the Son he loves" (Col. 1:13). Redeemed, we are armed for the fight to extend that kingdom and push back the forces of Satan. The fighting may be fierce, but we must not lose hope, for what we are waging is essentially a mop-up operation. Because of the Resurrection, the war has been won, the victory is assured.[2]

We need what C. S. Lewis called *mere Christianity*: collegiate believers standing together, rallying around the great truths of Scripture and the ancient creeds. Only when such unity is visible in the world will we truly experience the power of the gospel.

Then, standing together as the people of God, we must obey the two great commissions: first to win the lost and then to build a culture. Christians who are college students must seize this moment to show the world that Christianity is not only true . . . it is humanity's one great hope.

How do college students redeem a culture? How do we rise to the opportunity before us at the start of a new millennium?

The answer is simple: from the inside out. From the individual to friends to the community, and then outward in ever widening ripples. And we must begin by

understanding what it means to live by Christian worldview principles in our own behavior and choices. Unless we do, we will interpret the biblical commands according to the spirit of the age and will then be conformed to the world rather than to God's Word.

If we want to convert our pagan culture, we must start with ourselves, understanding what a Christian worldview means for our own moral and lifestyle choices.

What does it mean for us to redeem cultures from the inside out? _____
_____
_____

In a nutshell, if we reject the biblical teaching about creation, we end up with nature as our creator. Morality then becomes something students invent when they have evolved to a certain level. There is no transcendent source of moral standards that dictates how we should live. Each individual has the right to chart his or her own course.

By contrast, Christianity claims that God created the universe with a definite structure—a material order and a moral order.

What happens if we live contrary to that order? _____

On the other hand, if we submit to that order and live in harmony with it, then our lives will be happier and healthier. The role of public authorities is to encourage people to live according to the principles that make for social health and harmony.

Over the past three decades, these biblical concepts have receded while our public discourse has been dominated by the value-free model. Today, the disastrous consequences of that model have become abundantly clear. Even determined secularists have begun to see that society simply can't keep up with the costs of personal and moral irresponsibility.

There's a growing body of scientific evidence we can use to back up our argument. Medical studies are confirming that those who attend church regularly and act consistently with their faith are better off, both physically and mentally. Consider a few recent findings.

- *Alcohol Abuse:* Alcohol abuse is highest among those with little or no religious commitment.[3]
- *Drug Abuse:* Numerous studies have found an inverse correlation between religious commitment and drug abuse.
- *Crime:* There is also a strong correlation between participation in religious activities and the avoidance of crime.
- *Depression and Stress:* Several studies have found that high levels of religious commitment correlate with lower levels of depression and stress.[4]
- *Suicide:* Persons who do not attend church are four times more likely to commit suicide than are frequent church attenders. [5]
- *Mental Disorders:* Christians are far less likely to experience mental disorders than their secular counterparts. Why? Because "the one essential feature that characterizes all types of depression" is "the feeling of hopelessness and helplessness," and Christians are never without hope.[6]
- *Family Stability:* A number of studies have found a strong inverse correlation between church attendance and divorce, and one study found that church attendance is the most important predictor of marital stability.[7]
- *Marital and Sexual Satisfaction:* Churchgoers are more likely to say they would marry the same spouse again—an important measure of marital satisfaction.
- *Physical Health:* Studies have shown belonging to a religious group can lower blood pressure, relieve stress, and enhance survival after a heart attack.

How can faith on your campus affect the following concerns of our society? Can you give an answer to each one?
- **Alcohol Abuse**
- **Drug Abuse**
- **Crime**
- **Depression and Stress**
- **Suicide**
- **Mental Disorders**
- **Family Stability**
- **Marital and Sexual Satisfaction**
- **Physical Health**

This does not mean that every person of faith is healthy and happy, but the statistics do "make a powerful statement about the typical human condition," writes Patrick Glynn in *God: The Evidence*. Both clinical experience and research data suggest that "among the most important determinants of human happiness and well-being are our spiritual beliefs and moral choices."[8]

It is time for the medical profession to recognize the healing potential of the spiritual dimension, says Harvard professor Herbert Benson. Though not a professing Christian himself, Benson admits that humans are "engineered for religious faith." We are "wired for God. . . . Our genetic blueprint has made believing in an Infinite Absolute part of our nature."[9]

Benefits accrue only to those who practice their faith, not to those who merely profess it.

In short, the inconsistent Christian suffers even more than the consistent atheist. The most miserable person of all is the one who knows the truth, yet doesn't obey it.

We cannot escape the consequences of our own choices. In our bodies, we flesh out either the biblical worldview or a worldview that is in opposition to the Bible. And when we incarnate the truth of God in our lives and families, we help bring new life to our neighborhoods and churches, our cities and nation, in an ever widening circle.

Points to Remember

List two key points of today's session.

1. _____
   _____
2. _____
   _____

Questions to Ask

What questions do I have concerning what I've read today? _____
_____
_____
_____

Actions to Take

Based on what I've read, what specific action(s) should I take? _____
_____
_____

Prayers to Pray

Today, God, you taught me _____
_____
_____

Help me, Lord, to _____
_____

DAY TWO

A Marriage That will Endure

"Submit yourselves one to another in the fear of God" (Ephesians 5:21).

The Christian worldview teaches that from the beginning, God created individuals in relationship. By creating human beings as male and female, God established the interrelatedness of human sexuality, the marital relationship, and the institution of the family, each with its own divinely given moral norms.

As we move out from the range of individuals and their choices, the first circle of influence is in the intimate relationships of our friends. Nowhere is the clash of worldviews more pronounced than here. Nowhere are its effects more disastrous. Nowhere does it touch more deeply on the natural order that underlies all civilizations. And nowhere is it more evident that Christians must take a worldview approach if we are going to make a difference. Many believers have become politically active over issues, yet our efforts are usually reactive rather than proactive, largely because we have failed to confront the underlying worldview assumptions.

It's important that we cut through the rhetoric and get to the root of this conflict, which again hinges on our basic assumptions about creation, the Fall, and redemption. The Christian worldview teaches that from the beginning, God created individuals in relationship. By creating human beings as male and female, God established

the interrelatedness of human sexuality, the marital relationship, and the institution of the family, each with its own divinely given moral norms. While there can be great variety in the cultural expression of these institutions, when we enter into the covenant of marriage and family, we submit to an objective and God-given structure.

Briefly summarize what the Christian worldview teaches about marriage relationships. __
_____
_____
_____
_____

This radically changes one's view of marriage, for if it is not rooted in the way we were originally created, then it is something we can alter at our own will. What's more, all choices become morally equivalent, and there is no justification for favoring some choices over others. If someone wants a traditional marriage, that's fine. If someone else wants a same-sex marriage or some other variant, well, that's fine too.

Briefly summarize what the contemporary worldview teaches about marriage. _____
_____
_____
_____

In some circles, assuming that someone is married is now even an insult to them. What we're seeing is that challenges to traditional morality are themselves treated as moral crusades. For if no choices are wrong, then no lifestyle may be criticized and one must never be made to feel guilty.

This negative view of marriage has yielded consequences across the entire culture. If people dare to say that marriage is superior to other arrangements, they are accused of "discrimination." Many public schools today won't even consider a program that holds marriage up as an ideal.

Consider these statistics.

1. Children in single-parent families are six times more likely to be poor, and half the single mothers in the United States live below the poverty line.
2. Girls in single-parent homes are at much greater risk for precocious sexuality and are three times more likely to have a child out of wedlock.[10]
3. Crime and substance abuse are strongly linked to fatherless households.
4. Among two-thirds of divorced couples, one partner is still depressed and financially precarious. And among a quarter of all divorced couples, both former partners are worse off, suffering loneliness and depression.[11]
5. Children of divorce are more prone to illness, accidents, and suicide.
6. Divorced women lose 50 percent more time to illness and injury each year than do married women, and they are two to three times as likely to die of all forms of cancer.

7. Both divorced men and women are almost five times more likely to succumb to substance abuse.[12]
8. When family breakdown becomes widespread, entire neighborhoods decay. Neighborhoods without fathers are often infected with crime and delinquency.

Generation Xers often sense these truths better than their baby-boomer parents do. Many have suffered through their parents' divorce(s) and typically say they desperately hope for a marriage that will endure while at the same time they are profoundly pessimistic about marriage.

As a child of baby-boomer parents, what are your feelings about marriage? How hopeful are you? _____
_____
_____

The time is ripe for Christians to make a persuasive case for a biblical view of marriage and family, using statistics like these to frame a convincing argument that people are happier and healthier in stable families. And then we must learn how to model the biblical view before a watching world.

What does the Christian worldview say about the family? For most Christian students yet to marry, this information is invaluable. The doctrine of creation tells us God made us with a definite nature (in His image) and gave us a definite task: to nurture and develop the powers of nature (fill the earth and subdue it) and to form families and create societies (be fruitful and increase in number). The image of God is reflected, in part, in the differentiation of humanity into two sexes. "God created man in his own image . . . male and female he created them" (Gen. 1:27). The implication is that to be a husband or wife, a father or mother, is not an artificial or arbitrary role separate from our "true" self, a threat to authentic personhood. Instead, these relationships form an intrinsic part of our

The time is ripe for Christians to make a persuasive case for a biblical view of marriage and family, using statistics like these to frame a convincing argument that people are happier and healthier in stable families.

fundamental identity, of what makes us fully human. Liberation is not found by escaping these roles but by embracing them and carrying out our responsibilities in a manner faithful to God's ideals.

Identify some key biblical points about the family from the above paragraph. _____

_____

_____

_____

Biblical theology is expressed in marriage, with the faithful love between husband and wife as an image of God's faithful love for His people. In the New Testament, Paul likens the relationship between a husband and a wife to the "profound mystery" of Christ's union with His bride, the church (see Eph. 5).

As husband and wife come together, they form a family, the core institution of human society—the training ground, in fact, for all other social institutions. Human sexuality is not designed merely as a source of pleasure or a means of expressing affection. It was designed as a powerful bond between husband and wife in order to form a secure, stable environment for raising vulnerable children to adulthood. Family life is the "first school" that prepares us to participate in the religious, civic, and political life of society, training us in the virtues that enable us to place the common good before our own private goals. Saying no to sex outside marriage means saying yes to this broader vision of marriage as the foundation of an enduring institution that not only meets personal needs but also ties us into a wider community through mutual obligations and benefits.

Sadly, many local churches have been ineffective in sharing this message to college students. Their response to the decline of marriage has often been helpless hand-wringing and haranguing against a decadent culture. Few clergy have known how to put the brakes on the destructive trends

that have torn marriages apart at ever-increasing rates, even within their own congregations. One consequence is that 50 percent of the students on campus today come from broken homes.

What are some of the most important principles that churches can teach families? _____

_____

_____

_____

_____

For starters, collegiate believers should be encouraged to treat their own families as a ministry—a mission to the surrounding culture. Many friends of mine have this kind of vision for their families.

Another reality on campus is the "extended family." Although you don't turn your back on your biological family, when you think of family you think of special friendships being formed on campus as family. Whether this family is small or large, whether your resources are extensive or sparse, every Christian student is called to make the family a ministry. This means educating close friends in a biblical worldview and equipping them to have an impact on the world. In the long run, this is the best way that Christians can restore and redeem the surrounding culture.

The extended family is one arena where every collegiate Christian can and must be a redemptive force. Yet as you work to incorporate biblical principles within your extended family and even your biological family, you inevitably come up against the counterforce of public education. Nowhere has the secular worldview gained a firmer foothold than in our nation's universities, and since the education of college students shapes the future, collegiate Christians must begin to take our redemptive message right into the classrooms.

Clearly, American education is no longer successful at its two historic tasks: academic training and moral education.

How would you rate your own collegiate education in both of these areas?
Academic training: (Check one)
❏ excellent ❏ adequate ❏ so-so ❏ poor
Moral education: (Check one)
❏ excellent ❏ adequate ❏ so-so ❏ poor

Christian education should not assume that students are capable of determining ultimate truth on their own in the vacuum of subjectivism. Instead, God has communicated with us through the Bible, revealing an objective standard of truth and morality for all people. Our lives are guided by revealed truths that are much greater than anything we could possibly conceive on our own.

The Bible's Standard of Truth

First, students are not merely biological organisms adapting to the environment; they are created in the image of God and bear all the dignity of beings capable of recognizing truth, goodness, and beauty. The goal of education should be to feed students' souls based on these objective ideals.

Second, we must also take into account the capacity of students on campus for selfishness and willfulness. Informed by biblical standards, education should set firm behavioral limits on students and exert reasonable forms of discipline.

Third, education is one of the ways we seek to reverse the effects of the Fall and restore humanity to its original dignity and purpose.

What the colleges/universities do today determines what society will do tomorrow. As a Christian on the campus, you must be aware of the decline of education on all levels, from preschools to university campuses. Christians have an opportunity not only to have an influence on our public institutions but also to create Christian centers of education that will become sources of cultural renewal much as the monasteries did in the Middle Ages. Though secular-

ists once condemned biblical faith as irrational and contrary to reason, ironically Christianity now stands poised to become the great defender of reason.

Turn to Ephesians 5:21-6:4 and answer the following questions.
What word describes self-giving of one to the other? _____

1. **How is the wife to respond to her husband?** _____
_____
2. **How is the husband to respond to his wife?**
_____
_____

This model is one for the future if you are not already married as a student.

✔ Points to Remember
List two key points of today's session.
1. _____
_____
2. _____
_____

❓ Questions to Ask
What questions do I have concerning what I've read today? _____
_____
_____

👥 Actions to Take
Based on what I've read, what specific action(s) should I take? _____
_____
_____

✳ Prayers to Pray
Today, God, you taught me _____
_____
_____
_____

Help me, Lord, to _____
_____
_____

> *God has communicated with us through the Bible, revealing an objective standard of truth and morality for all people.*

To Live In Community

"Therefore, since we are surrounded by such a great cloud of witnesses, let us throw off everything that hinders and the sin that so easily entangles, and let us run with perseverance the race marked out for us" (Hebrews 12:1).

But it isn't just insufficient manpower and firepower that allows crime to flourish. It is also a flawed worldview.

When people live together according to God's moral order—in shalom—there is civility and harmony.

God has created us as inherently communal beings, and the God-ordained institutions of society make rightful demands that we are morally obligated to fulfill.

Over the past few decades, both crime and public disorder have risen sharply. The resulting social chaos has turned America's inner cities into combat zones, and nothing seems able to stop the downward spiral.

What would you say to be the main reason for crime?

Many people blame our inability to respond to crime effectively on the fact that in many cities the police are outnumbered and outgunned. But it isn't just insufficient manpower and firepower that allows crime to flourish. It is also a flawed worldview.

If we hope to restore our cities, we must understand and critique the worldview that unleashed this disorder. This novel view of civil liberties was the direct result of the same philosophy we've described before, rejection of the biblical doctrine of creation and replacing the garden of Eden with a hypothetical "state of nature."

Thousands of years ago, the Jewish people had already captured the idea for a solution in *shalom*. Although popularly translated "peace," the connotations of the term are actually much broader than the absence of hostilities. Shalom refers to peace in a positive sense, the result of a rightly ordered community. When people live together according to God's moral order—in shalom—there is civility and harmony. Hence, the best way to reduce crime is not

to react after the fact with punishments and rehabilitation but to discourage it before it happens by creating an ordered and civil community life.

The biblical basis for this approach is the doctrine of creation, which tells us we were created for community. Contrary to the notion of a "state of nature," with its war of all against all, the Bible teaches that we are not autonomous individuals. Instead, we are created in the image of the One "who in His very essence is a community of being"—that is, the Trinity. God's very nature is reciprocal love and communication between the persons of the Trinity. God has created us as inherently communal beings, and the God-ordained institutions of society make rightful demands that we are morally obligated to fulfill.

Think of one or more ways how this (shalom) can affect crime. Jot down your thoughts.

For centuries this biblical view of communal order dominated Western thought.

The success that this approach has exhibited in restoring America's major cities underlines the wisdom of the classic biblical view and provides powerful evidence that it is, in fact, true—true to our nature, true to who we are. The chaos of the last few decades attests to the disastrous consequences of living by a false philosophy of human nature, one that denies the biblical teaching of creation and substitutes a secular myth of our origins and our nature. The secular view has been tried and found wanting, and its failure opens a wonderful opportunity for Christians to make a case for a biblical view of human nature and community.

The good news is that we also have positive evidence that the Christian view really works.

One of the most successful examples is Charleston, South Carolina, where Police Chief Reuben Greenberg decided to fight crime by cleaning up inner-city neighborhoods, getting rid of litter, used needles, and graffiti. To keep costs down, he employed prisoners from the local jail. Soon formerly crime-ridden areas were clean and neat, signaling that disruptive and disorderly behavior would not be tolerated.

Even students can get in on the act. A few years ago, in Montgomery, Alabama, fifty Christian teenagers armed with hedge clippers and weed whackers descended on a neighborhood of mostly elderly people, determined to tackle the overgrown bushes that provided hiding places for vandals, burglars, and muggers. The kids trimmed towering hedges, thinned low-hanging tree branches, even replaced burned-out lights and installed peepholes in doors.

Why do you think establishing order works so well as a crime preventive? _____
_____
_____

Because it expresses an underlying moral order and shows that the community is willing to enforce it.

In fact, it is only Christians who have a worldview capable of providing workable solutions to the problems of community life. Thus, collegiate Christians ought to be in the forefront, helping communities take charge of their own neighborhoods. Whether it's mobilizing efforts to paint over graffiti and clean up vacant lots, or whether it's political activism to pass laws enforcing standards of public behavior, we should be helping to restore order in these smaller areas as the first step toward tackling major social ills.

Although our citizenship is in the City of God, we know that God has placed us in our cities and neighborhoods to reflect His character and to restore His righteous dominion in the midst of a fallen world. We begin with our personal lives and habits, move out from there to our friends and campus, and then into our communities–and from there into our society as a whole.

What would the following groups on your campus say to how we are to achieve the good life?
Athletes: _____

Social Clubs: _____
_____

Academic Crowd: _____
_____

Service Clubs: _____
_____

The same critical question, then, confronts us as we move beyond our friends and campus to consider our common life together: How can we achieve the virtue necessary to maintain a good society and to preserve liberty?

And how do the worldview categories of creation, fall, and redemption help us analyze the false views we confront in our culture today?

Creation tells us that we owe our existence to a holy God, whose character is the standard of all righteousness, the measure of all morality. "Be holy because I, the Lord your God, am holy" (Lev. 19:2). The clear failing of the secular worldview is that it tells us we owe our existence to natural forces acting at random; therefore, there can be no ultimate source of moral norms.

The second category is just as crucial. The Fall tells us we are prone to evil and

Christianity gives an absolute moral law that allows us to judge between right and wrong.

Only the Christian worldview offers redemption from sin, giving power to overcome the single most powerful obstacle to becoming virtuous: the rebellious human will.

At the heart of Christianity is a supernatural transforming power that enables us not only to know what is right but also to do it—to become virtuous.

thus need moral restraints for society to function. "What comes out of a man is what makes him 'unclean'" (Mark 7:20). But secularism fails to understand the nature of our moral dilemma. A virtuous society can be created only by virtuous people, wherein each individual's conscience guards the person's behavior and holds him or her accountable. Without conscience, a society can be held in check only through coercion. Yet even coercion ultimately fails, for there is no police force large enough to keep an eye on every individual. Christianity gives an absolute moral law that allows us to judge between right and wrong.

Try asking your secular friends how they decide what they ought to do, what ethical principles to follow. Write your responses in the margin.
How do they know those principles are right? _____
_____
On what authority do they rely? _____
_____

Without moral absolutes, there is no real basis for ethics. An absolute moral law doesn't confine people in a straitjacket of Victorian prudery. People will always debate the boundaries of moral law and its varied applications. But the very idea of right and wrong makes sense only if there is a final standard, a measuring rod, by which we can make moral judgments.

Only the Christian worldview offers redemption from sin, giving power to overcome the single most powerful obstacle to becoming virtuous: the rebellious human will. Morality is not just about an intellectual acknowledgment of ultimate standards, of what ought to be; morality is also about developing virtue—that is, the full range of habits and dispositions that constitute good character. We must not merely assent mentally to certain principles; we must become people who are just, coura-

geous, patient, kind, loyal, loving, persistent, and devoted to duty. And only the Christian worldview tells us how to develop virtuous character, to become moral persons.

What does the Old Testament prophet Jeremiah say about the heart in Jeremiah 17:9? _____
_____

What does the apostle Paul say about his "sinful nature" in Romans 7:18-19? _____
_____

I can testify to this from personal experience. In 1969, when President Nixon asked me to leave my lucrative law practice to serve as his special counsel, I saw it as my duty to do so, even though it meant a drastic pay cut. To guard against temptation, or even the appearance of impropriety, I put my law firm investment and all other assets into a blind trust and vowed never even to see former law partners or clients (who might seek government favors). I was determined: No one would corrupt me. Yet I went to prison for obstruction of justice.

What happened?

My problem was that I didn't understand the deceptiveness of the human heart. In college, I had studied the best of the world's moral philosophy, including Immanuel Kant's famous "categorical imperative," which is really a modified Golden Rule. So I knew well enough what was right. The problem was that I lacked the will to do it.

When we turn to God, the Holy Spirit empowers us to do what we cannot do on our own. This is the essence of the term *conversion*: the will is turned around; it is transformed. At the heart of Christianity is a supernatural transforming power that enables us not only to know what is right but also to do it—to become virtuous.

Although only a converted will is capable of virtue in a consistent manner, there is also a natural virtue spoken of in Romans 2 (conscience), which is a consequence of our creation in the image of God. And while Christians must work for the conversion of individuals, we also have a duty to help create a good society by cultivating ethical knowledge even among the unconverted.

Our most intractable social problems cannot be solved by public policies but only by the practice of virtuous behavior. The way societies encourage virtuous behavior is positively through custom and convention, and negatively through social stigmas, taboos, and shame. Admittedly, the latter are difficult to exert in a culture where no moral stigma is permitted for fear of damaging someone's self-esteem. But as a Christian student, you can cut through this fog and argue for the right of a healthy society to express moral disapproval of socially harmful behavior.

Now, answer this question yourself. What does it take to create the good life?

_____

_____

_____

From what you studied today, you could write . . . "a firm sense of right and wrong, and a determination to order one's life accordingly." Not out of a grim sense of duty, but because it is what fits with our created nature and makes us happiest and most fulfilled. [13]

When we know the secret to true happiness, we will seek virtue in every area of life, even those that are typically thought to be purely technical or scientific or utilitarian. And when that happens, we will make the astonishing discovery that the Christian worldview is vital for our economic well-being and gives genuine meaning even to our work.

Turn to Hebrews 12:1-12 and answer the following questions.

What does the writer of Hebrews encourage us to do?_____

_____

Who should we keep our eyes on?

_____

Why does the Lord discipline us? _____

_____

What will discipline produce?

_____

✅ Points to Remember
List two key points of today's session.
1. _____

_____

2. _____

_____

❓ Questions to Ask
What questions do I have concerning what I've read today? _____

_____

_____

👥 Actions to Take
Based on what I've read, what specific action(s) should I take? _____

_____

_____

✴ Prayers to Pray
Today, God, you taught me _____

_____

_____

_____

_____

_____

Help me, Lord, to_____

_____

_____

_____

_____

Changing the Culture

DAY FOUR
Law and Order

"He who has been stealing must steal no longer, but must work, doing something useful with his own hands, that he may have something to share with those in need" (Ephesians 4:28).

In the first centuries after Christ, the early church was forced to define a biblical view of work and economic development in contrast to the views inherited from ancient Greek culture, which equated the material world with evil and disorder.

God's Word has a great deal to say about work; and although the Bible may not endorse any particular economic theory, it also lays out a basic blueprint for a society that is free, prosperous, and just. A Christian worldview perspective on work and economic development clearly follows the basic contours of the categories of *creation, fall,* and *redemption.* In the opening chapters of Genesis, we learn that human beings were made in the image of God, to reflect His character; therefore, we are called to reflect His creative activity through our own creativity—by cultivating the world, drawing out its potential, and giving it shape and form. All work has dignity as an expression of the divine image.

Turning to the testimony of history, we can trace a steady development in the dignity accorded to the individual and to eco-nomic vocation. In the first centuries after Christ, the early church was forced to define a biblical view of work and economic development in contrast to the views inherited from ancient Greek culture, which equated the material world with evil and disorder. Against this backdrop . . .

(1) The early church defended a high view of the material world as God's creation.

(2) Thomas Aquinas stressed the value of the created world.

(3) The Reformers protested vigorously against the dichotomy between the sacred secular and its implicit devaluation of creation.

(4) The division into sacred and secular had not only made secular work second-best but also held secular workers to a lower standard of devotion and spirituality.

(5) The Reformation challenged that, insist-

Read the following Scriptures and match each with its appropriate response.

_____ Genesis 2:15	A. Condemnation on those who manipulate the economy for their own sinful purposes.
_____ Job 42:10-12	B. Those who refuse to work should earn the food they eat.
_____ 1 Timothy 6:10	C. Those who incur a debt are to be prompt in repayment.
_____ Psalm 24:1	D. Work the earth and take care of it.
_____ Amos 5:11-12	E. Wealth can lead to spiritual complacency and even disobedience to God.
_____ Proverbs 3:27-28	G. Share with the hungry.
_____ Psalm 37:21	H. Wealth can be a reward for spiritual faithfulness.
_____ Isaiah 58:7	I. God will judge those who take advantage of the needy.
_____ 2 Thessalonians 3:11-12	J. Care for the widows.
_____ Acts 6:1	K. God owns it all.

ing that no believer is exempt from the highest spiritual standards.

Which point is closest to your view of work? Why? _____
_____
_____

These beliefs about the value of work and entrepreneurial talent shaped what became known as the Protestant work ethic. This, in turn, became the driving force behind the industrial revolution, which has raised the standard of living immeasurably for vast numbers of societies around the globe. The impact of the work ethic is one of the great examples of the way a Christian worldview can revolutionize a culture.

This is a major issue facing Christians in this area. How do we transform a secularized, demoralized capitalism into a morally responsible free-market system?

The most important point we need to make is that an economy is not an autonomous mechanism.

It depends, first of all, on a juridical framework: on a system of laws to maintain a sound currency, protect private property, enforce contracts, and clamp down on corruption. Government acts as a referee, making sure everyone follows the rules and plays fair.

Humane capitalism also depends on a sound moral culture, for a free market readily caters to the moral choices we make, supplying whatever consumers want—from Bibles to pornography.

And we now know there are simply no shortcuts: Morality in the marketplace depends on each individual economic actor. This is why the Christian's role is indispensable, for we alone have the resources to help create a healthy moral climate.

All this can be summed up by saying that economic success depends on morality. As societies around the world shake off the chains of communism and socialism, it is more imperative than ever that

Christians make a case for the moral and spiritual basis of a free economy. If a thoroughly secularized capitalism is adopted, it will surely lead not to freedom but to new forms of slavery, just as early capitalism created its "dark satanic mills." Capitalism provides the best opportunity for economic growth and human freedom only if it is tempered by compassion and social justice.

Defend the statement that "economic success depends on morality." _____
_____
_____
_____
_____
_____

For many Americans, with weakened ties to family and church, the workplace has become the primary social environment. Coworkers have become the new family, the tribe, the social world. Many corporations consciously seek to become the center of employees' lives, offering child care, health centers, drug and alcohol counseling, and an array of social services.

All this is symptomatic, however, of a more fundamental problem—which is that many students have lost a sense of a higher purpose for work. Work no longer has a transcendent purpose as a means of serving and loving God. No wonder, then, that many students are questioning the very meaning of work.

This offers Christians a rich opportunity to make the case that work is truly fulfilling only when firmly tied to its moral and spiritual moorings. It is time for the church to reclaim this crucial part of life, restoring a biblical understanding of work and economics. A biblical theology of work should be a frequent subject for sharing with others on campus. Christian college students should organize classes on business ethics and biblical work principles for those going into the workplace.

The impact of the work ethic is one of the great examples of the way a Christian worldview can revolutionize a culture.

All this can be summed up by saying that economic success depends on morality.

> *Christianity even gives us the basic presuppositions needed to run a nation through just and fair-minded laws, and to foster a political system that is both free and well ordered.*

Your business class has just been asked by the university to set up such a program. Create a program to propose to your professor/pastor. Consider the following:
• Purpose/Mission Statement
• Leadership Needed
• Training Available
• Budget Available
• Location of Program
• Community Involvement Needed

_____
_____
2. _____
_____
_____
3. _____
_____
_____
4. _____
_____

Christianity even gives us the basic presuppositions needed to run a nation through just and fair-minded laws, and to foster a political system that is both free and well ordered.

The Christian understanding of law as based on a higher moral law has parallels in most civilizations throughout history. As C. S. Lewis pointed out, all major religions and moral systems assume the existence of an objective morality (which he called the Way or the Tao).[14]

The consequences of this are shaking the very foundations of our government and society today.

First, the loss of moral authority in the law removes restraints on individual behavior.

Second, the loss of moral authority in the law means government is reduced to utilitarian procedures.

Third, the loss of a moral basis for law means we can no longer engage in moral debate.

Fourth, the loss of moral authority in the law means we have forfeited the rule of law and reverted to arbitrary human rule.

Yet we must not give up hope, for Christian truth still offers us a way out of the postmodernist impasse. Christians everywhere can help revitalize our political culture and reestablish the rule of law by advancing a biblical view of law and politics.

List these four consequences of a secular worldview of law.

1. _____

If we have learned anything in recent decades, it is that we should not roll out heavy-handed political movements that recklessly toss around "God-and-country" clichés and scare off our secular neighbors. Our goal is not to grab power and impose our views. Instead, we should act through principled persuasion and responsible participation.

Persuasion means our first task is apologetics—striving to convince our neighbors that the Christian worldview provides the best way to order society. We can assume most of our neighbors do not understand the necessity of even something so basic as the rule of law.

We also need to press home the importance of the idea of the common good. Take the illustration of a stoplight: For the public good, all people are required to stop at stoplights; otherwise there would be chaos and death on the streets.

We need to apply the same reasoning to other laws, such as those recognizing marriage only between two persons of the opposite sex. There are important reasons why protecting heterosexual marriage is in the interest of society: It recognizes a social pattern that every civilized society has adopted in order to propagate the human race and raise children. Christians need to argue that such laws do not "impose" a religious belief but are based on rational moral principles and historical evidence showing that protection of the family promotes the public interest.

Finally, we can argue that the Christian

worldview provides the most reliable standard for determining the public good and encouraging responsible personal behavior. Perhaps the toughest sell today is persuading people that they ought to govern their personal behavior for the public good. We need to argue that unless individuals voluntarily restrain their own behavior for the common good, government will have to restrain them by coercive measures—at the cost of our liberty.

We must also make the case by the way we live. Others will see the truth of what we believe most clearly if we live out our convictions as responsible students on our campuses.

First, we live out our convictions when we are good citizens. The most elementary requirement of any society is that its citizens behave responsibly, obey the law, and carry out their civic duties. Christians should be the best of citizens, as Augustine said, because we do out of love for God what others do only because they are forced to by law. This means that we vote, don't cheat, care for our campuses, and live peaceably with others. We honor and obey our leaders and civil magistrates, and we pray for those in authority.

Second, we live out our convictions when we do our civic duty in every walk of life. People may make light of the "Jesus Saves" banner across the door of the mission shelters and soup kitchens, but they can't deny that these places are dispensing mercy and compassion to the destitute. Visit our inner cities, and you will discover the Salvation Army, gospel missions, and other religious charities provide the vast majority of private relief services. In poverty-stricken areas, organizations like Habitat for Humanity are building homes and providing other relief for the poor.

Third, we live out our convictions when we are engaged in politics. Christians should exercise diligently the opportunities available for shaping the political process. It includes joining civic groups and political organizations, and perhaps even running for public office. Christian organizations active in politics need to set distinctively Christian goals and be uncompromising in biblical fidelity, never allowing themselves to be in the hip pocket of any political party. This is a narrow line to walk, but it can be done.

Fourth, we live out our convictions when we as Christian students act as the conscience of society, as a restraining influence against the misuse of governing authority. Corporately, the church must zealously guard its independence, keep its prophetic voice sharp, and resist the allure of worldly power. It should hold government morally accountable to live up to its delegated authority from God (along with holding all other spheres of society accountable to fulfill the functions ordained to them by God).

In addressing the state, we must do so not on the basis of power, as special interests do, but on the basis of principle. This is a crucial distinction, yet it is one that secular politicians and journalists frequently miss.

So our message is not, "We put you in office, now pay up." Rather, we are saying, This should be done because it is right, because it is a principle that undergirds any well-ordered civil society, and because it is a proper duty of the state ordained by God.

All this can be summed up by saying we should exhibit the best of Christian patriotism, always holding dear our land and nation while always holding it up against the standard of divine justice. If it is to remain so, we must be at our posts, "the king's good citizens but the Lord's first." We must always be ready to show our fellow students the way to restore truth and moral authority to American law and politics.

Turn to Ephesians 4:17-32 and answer the following questions.

1. Paul contrasted the way of the Gentiles and that of Christians as the difference between _____ and light.

2. What were the believers taught?

_____

_____

3. What does Paul say is one reason for working? _____

_____

4. What specific actions does Paul encourage the believers to do? _____

_____

_____

_____

✔ Points to Remember
List two key points of today's session.

1. _____

_____

2. _____

_____

❓ Questions to Ask
What questions do I have concerning what I've read today? _____

_____

_____

_____

👤 Actions to Take
Based on what I've read, what specific action(s) should I take? _____

_____

_____

_____

_____

✷ Prayers to Pray
Today, God, you taught me _____

_____

_____

_____

_____

_____

_____

Help me, Lord, to _____

_____

_____

_____

_____

DAY FIVE
Lead the Way

"In the same way, let your light shine before men, that they may see your good deeds and praise your Father in heaven" (Matthew 5:16).

The task for Christian students is clear: to expose the flaws in scientific materialism, which has invested science with ultimate intellectual authority. This is our task not because we are against science but because we want to restore science to its proper role as a means of investigating God's world and improving the lot of His people. Christians collegians can lead the way because the original conception of science was developed in the context of the biblical worldview, and only in that context can it function properly.

The method of investigation that we now know as modern science first emerged in Christianized Europe, a culture steeped in biblical faith, and most of the key figures in the scientific revolution were Christians, working from a basis of faith. In fact, contemporary historians of science, both

Christians and non-Christians, agree that Christianity provided the underlying attitudes and intellectual presuppositions that made modern science possible. Some of the most important were:

1. The physical world is real, not an illusion. Most Eastern cultures embrace pantheism, which teaches that the physical world is an illusion (maya).

2. Nature is good but not divine. Another mistaken view comes from pagan animism, which teaches that the world is the abode of the divine or an emanation of God's own essence; animism asserts that nature is alive with sun gods, river goddesses, and astral deities.

3. Nature is orderly and predictable. Another unique contribution of Christianity was the idea of laws of nature.

4. The order in nature is mathematically precise. Modern science depends on the idea that the order in nature is precise and can be expressed in mathematical formulas. This, too, was a contribution of Christianity.

From the list of these four attitudes and presuppositions, write the appropriate number besides its biblical truth.

____ **God created the material world.**
____ **Nature is God's handiwork.**
____ **The world comes completely from God's hand.**
____ **God is both Creator and law giver.**

Our first goal in dealing with schools, then, should be to get educators to separate philosophical claims from scientific theories. In other words, we must get them to stop treating philosophical statements as if they were science.

Second, we should press for teaching science honestly. Educators should teach not only the examples that confirm evolution but also those that contradict it, the anomalies and unsolved questions.

Third, perhaps the most important thing we can do is encourage Christian young people to go into science as a profession and demonstrate the viability of a biblical framework for science. We need more college students making the decision, "I've been thinking, I can be a missionary as a microbiologist." If we are going to craft a winning strategy for extending Christ's lordship over all of life, we need missionaries in science and every other discipline and vocation.

God calls us to "demolish arguments and every pretension that sets itself up against the knowledge of God," and to "take captive every thought to make it obedient to Christ" (2 Cor.10:5). We must not fail to heed this call when it comes to modern science, for otherwise there's no telling what "compelling" but false new myths scientists may concoct to feed our society's deep spiritual hunger.

The reformation of science—and the way we think about reality—is not just a matter for ivory-tower academicians. It affects our entire worldview—not only ideas about religion and ethics but also about the arts, music, and popular culture.

For the Christian, the arts are also an important way to understand God and His creation, for the arts give us ears to hear and eyes to see more clearly. Artists are gifted with a special sensitivity to the glories of creation, and through their work, they can bring these glories into sharper focus for others.[15] The principle is simple: When God created the world, He cared enough to make it beautiful. There is no more convincing argument that God Himself is pleased with beauty than to gaze at the delicate hues of a wildflower against dark green moss, the blue expanse of a Montana sky, the sharp outlines of the Rockies. What's more, when God communicated His Word to us, He did so in a variety of literary styles: history, poetry, liturgical formulas, ethical principles, hymns, letters, maxims and proverbs, and even a love song.

Since God made human beings in His

image, our capacity for aesthetic enjoyment is part of the way He created us—one of His good gifts to us. "One thing I ask of the Lord," says the psalmist. "That I may . . . gaze upon the beauty of the Lord" (Ps. 27:4).

What is one of your favorite artistic enjoyments? _____

Understood in a biblical context, of course, there is nothing wrong with claiming that human creativity reflects the creativity of God, in whose image we are made. But torn out of that context, the notion quickly became idolatrous. In defending their work, artists began to overcompensate by claiming that art is actually superior to science. They insisted that the imagination, not scientific reason, is most like God; art finds its highest form not in representing reality but in creating something completely new and imaginary. Thus the artist became idolized, and art itself became a surrogate for religion.

To make the campus community a godly culture, we must start by finding ways to reconnect with our own literary and artistic heritage. Go to concerts, read classic literature, visit art museums. Get to know the composers, writers, and painters who have been inspired by Christian faith. Enjoy the arts not only as art but also as media that speak to us spiritually.

Christians should also be familiar with contemporary writers. Among fiction writers, every Christian should explore the riches of C. S. Lewis, especially his space trilogy and Narnia stories and the fantasy of J.R.R. Tolkien, especially his incomparable *Lord of the Rings* trilogy.

Visual artists, too, have expressed the classic Christian faith in modern forms. Among twentieth-century painters, some of the most beautiful and tender works have been rendered by Georges Rouault, who as an adult became an evangelical Catholic.

Corporately, your campus and other Christian students can take a role in supporting the arts by involving artists in religious services: invite musicians to write and play music; ask poets and writers to create dramatic presentations for religious holidays; encourage artists to design banners and bulletins and other works of beauty for the secular eye. If you belong to a religious organization on campus, you could sponsor a Christian artists show and begin to penetrate the secular worldview on campus.

Could this be a trip to the library or art gallery on campus to discover more about ways God is seen? Think about it!

By voting with our dollars, over time as a Christian on the campus, you can also make a difference in what's offered on the campus related to the Arts. Refuse to attend musical concerts you know will be filled with obscene or indecent lyrics. Protest to the administration concerning movies that glorify immorality and are paid for by your student fees. Refuse to buy romance novels that cheapen the relationship between men and women and even border on soft porn. Taking a stand—whether organized or merely individual—may not always get a product taken off the market, but you make an important moral statement.

The best way to overcome banality on campus is to cultivate something better. We must seek out, as Paul writes in Philippians, "whatever is true, whatever is noble, whatever is right, whatever is pure, whatever is lovely, whatever is admirable—if anything is excellent or praiseworthy—think about such things" (Phil. 4:8). Notice that Paul doesn't limit that principle to spiritual things. The campus administration is listening!

Ultimately, though, to be a redemptive force in popular culture, we must encourage Christians to go beyond being critical and start being creative. Look for new forms which glorify God.

Consider the type of Christian music you listen to. List an artist and evaluate their music according to its content and style.

Artist :_____

Content: _____

_____

In popular culture, as in every field, the best way to reach a non-believing audience is not so much by works that preach Christianity explicitly as by works that express a Christian worldview indirectly. "We can make people attend to the Christian point of view for half an hour or so," said C. S. Lewis, "but the moment they have gone away from our lecture or laid down the article, they are plunged back into a world where the opposite position is taken for granted." Therefore, "What we want is not more little books about Christianity, but more little books by Christians on other subjects—with their Christianity latent."[16]

What would happen . . .
- **if the best popular music on the market were composed by Christian musicians?**
- **If the best books in the bookstores were written by Christian authors?**
- **If the best television shows implicitly communicated a Christian worldview?**

Non-believers would quickly see that Christianity is not something that can be relegated to a separate part of life labeled "religion" but is a viable worldview that makes better sense of all the things they care about.

Does the devil have all the good music? By our choices, you and I can make sure he doesn't.

As we have sought to demonstrate in these pages, the Christian worldview is more consistent, more rational, and more workable than any other belief system.
- It beats out all other contenders in giving credible answers to the great questions that any worldview must answer: Where did we come from? (creation); What is the

human dilemma? (fall); and What can we do to solve the dilemma? (redemption). As a result, the way we see the world will lead to changing the world (restoration).
- No worldview is merely a theoretical philosophy; worldview is intensely practical.
- It affects the way we live our lives, day in and day out, as well as the way we influence the world around us.
- If we order our lives in accord with reality, we will not only find meaning and purpose but also discover that our lives are healthier and more fulfilled. Christianity is that road map of reality, and it is the answer we must be ready to give as those around us grow increasingly aware of the futility of all other worldviews.

But you say, can we ever hope to solve, or even help to solve, the intractable problems that set nation against nation?

The answer is that God uses acts of faith and faithfulness to heal the ugliest wounds and reconcile the deepest conflicts.

Turn to Matthew 5:13-16 and answer the following questions.

1. **Matthew refers to Christians as being _____ and _____.**

2. **As "light," to whom do we have responsibility? _____**

3. **Our lives should be a witness of what?**

_____
_____
_____
_____

4. **What is the end result of our testimony and influence?_____**

_____
_____
_____
_____
_____

Non-believers would quickly see that Christianity is not something that can be relegated to a separate part of life labeled "religion" but is a viable worldview that makes better sense of all the things they care about.

✅ Points to Remember

List two key points of today's session.

1. _____

_____

2. _____

_____

❓ Questions to Ask

What questions do I have concerning what I've read today? _____

_____

_____

_____

🫂 Actions to Take

Based on what I've read, what specific action(s) should I take? _____

_____

_____

_____

✳️ Prayers to Pray

Today, God, you taught me _____

_____

_____

_____

_____

_____

Help me, Lord, to _____

_____

_____

_____

_____

_____

_____

[1] Abraham Kuyper, *Christianity: A Total World and Life System* (Marlborough, N.H.:Plymouth Rock Foundation, 1996).

[2] See Al Wolters, *Creation Regained: Biblical Basis for a Reformational Worldview* (Grand Rapids:Eerdmans, 1985), chapter 4; and Charles Colson with Ellen Santilli Vaughn, *Kingdoms in Conflict*, (New York: William Morrow; Grand Rapids: Zondervan, 1987), chapter 7.

[3] D.B. Larson and W.P. Wilson "Religious Life of Alcoholics," *Southern Medical Journal* 73, no. 6 (June 1980): 723-27.

[4] David B. and Susan S. Larson, *The Forgotten Factor in Physical and Mental Health: What Does the Research Show?* (Rockville, MD.: National Institute for Healthcare Research, 1992), 76-78.

[5] Ibid., 64-65.

[6] Armand Nicholi Jr., "Hope in a Secular Age," *Finding God at Harvard: Spiritual Journeys of Thinking Christians*, ed. Kelly K. Monroe (Grand Rapids: Zondervan, 1996), 117.

[7] Larson and Larson, *The Forgotten Factor*, 72.

[8] Patrick Glynn, *God: The Evidence: The Reconciliation of Faith and Reason in a Postsecular World* (Rocklin, Calif.: Prima Publishing, 1997), 67.

[9] Herbert Benson, *Timeless Healing* (New York: Scribner, 1996), 197, 208.

[10] Michael McManus, "Voters Should Care about Divorce Reform," *Detroit News*, 19 September 1996.

[11] Judith S. Wallerstein and Sandra Blakeslee, *Second Chances: Men, Women, and Children a Decade after Divorce* (New York: Ticknor & Fields, 1989), 21-31.

[12] James L. Lynch, *The Broken Heart: The Medical Consequences of Loneliness in America* (New York: Basic Books, 1977), 69-86, 87-90, 41-50, appendix B.

[13] Deal W. Hudson, *Happiness and the Limits of Satisfaction* (Lanham, Md.: Rowman and Littlefield, 1996).

[14] See C. S. Lewis, *The Abolition of Man* (New York: Touchstone, 1975) and Mere Christianity (New York: Touchstone, 1996).

[15] Calvin Seerveld, interview with Nancy R. Pearcey, "Christianity and the Arts," *Perspective* 18, no. 3 (June 1984). See also Calvin Seerveld, *A Christian Critique of Art and Literature* (Toronto: Tuppence Press, 1995).

[16] C.S. Lewis, *God in the Dock: Essays on Theology and Ethics* (Grand Rapids: Eerdmans, 1970), 93.

The Magic School Bus

and the Climate Challenge

In memory of Craig Walker,
whose brilliant vision for making science exciting
and funny inspired the Magic School Bus series—
and both of us.
He was much loved, and is much missed.
—J.C. and B.D.

The Magic School Bus

and the Climate Challenge

By Joanna Cole

Illustrated by Bruce Degen

RECYCLED PAPER

Scholastic Inc.

Many have helped in the making of this book. In particular, our sincere thanks go to

Dr. Bill Chameides, Dean and Nicholas Professor of the Environment, Duke University,

for his enthusiastic and informed review.

This book was originally published in hardcover by Scholastic Press in 2010.

ISBN 978-0-545-65599-6

12 11 10 9   20 21 22/0

Printed in the U.S.A. 40
This edition first printing, January 2014

The text type was set in 15-point Bookman Light.
The illustrator used pen and ink, watercolor, color pencil, and gouache for the paintings in this book.
The text of this book prints on 100% post-consumer recycled fiber.

To all our friends in Korea.
We will never forget your warm and enthusiastic
welcome to The Magic School Bus, and to us.
— J.C. and B.D.

WELCOME, JOON

OUR VISITOR FROM SOUTH KOREA

Have you heard about our teacher, Ms. Frizzle? Almost every day, something weird happens in her class.

For example, take the day we started to study global warming. We were going to put on a play about Earth and all the changes that are happening.

The Friz had brought a book from home, and we were using the pictures to help us paint the scenery.

7

WHAT IS GLOBAL WARMING?
by Carlos

Global warming is a rise in the average temperature of the land and water on Earth. Today, the average temperature is more than 1 degree F warmer than it was 100 years ago.

One degree doesn't sound like much, but one small degree has caused big changes already— ice melting, seas rising, and more freak weather!

"Ms. Frizzle's book is kind of old," said Tim. "It came out before things really started heating up." "I'll go online to get new pictures," said Wanda. She headed for a computer, but Ms. Frizzle was already out the door. "Come on, class," she called. "Bring my book, please."

LET'S GET REALLY UP-TO-DATE INFORMATION.

I HATE IT WHEN SHE SAYS STUFF LIKE THAT.

WELL, I'VE HEARD HER NAME IS VALERIE....

BUT I CAN'T BELIEVE SHE WAS EVER NINE!

LET'S GO!

OUR WONDERFUL WORLD

This book belongs to Valerie Frizzle age 9.

Before you could say "North Pole,"
the Friz herded us onto the bus.
She pushed a few buttons and pulled a few levers.
Then we were on our way to the Arctic Sea—
a place with a completely different climate.

When we got there, Dorothy Ann opened
Ms. Frizzle's old book.
The pictures showed ice everywhere.
There was still plenty of ice in the Arctic,
but a lot had melted, and more
was melting all the time.

MELTING CAUSES MORE MELTING
by Tim

Ice is white. White reflects most of the sunlight that hits it. So the sun can't heat up the ice.

Water is not white. It absorbs most of the sunlight that hits it. So the water gets warmer.

This starts a dangerous loop:
• The warm water melts more ice.
• That means there is more water.
• This water takes in more sunlight.
• So the water gets warmer and melts even more ice.

And so on, and so on, until all the ice is gone.

HOW IT LOOKS NOW

IN THE ARCTIC, AN AREA HAS MELTED THAT'S THE SIZE OF TEXAS AND CALIFORNIA COMBINED!

Ms. Frizzle steered the bus-plane
all over the earth.
We saw changes everywhere.

5. Warming causes stronger hurricanes and tornadoes...

...and more forest fires...

...and bigger blizzards.

GLOBAL WARMING PUTS MORE WATER IN THE AIR IN SOME PLACES. THAT MEANS MORE RAIN, AND, WHEN IT GETS COLD, MORE SNOW!

WHY IS THERE STILL COLD WEATHER?
by Keesha
Global warming means that the average temperature of the whole earth is rising.
Different places still have different weather, but, in most places, there are more hot days and fewer cold days than before.

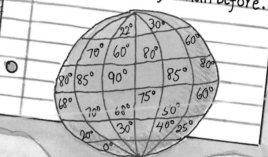

6. It causes animals and plants to die or to move.

IT'S TOO HOT HERE.

LET'S GO NORTH.

FIRE ANTS

YELLOW-BELLIED MARMOTS

7. Strange weather hurts food crops.

ICE ON AVOCADOS

THAT WHOLE CROP MIGHT BE LOST!

NO AVOCADOS? HOLY GUACAMOLE!

"Most of today's warming is caused by the increasing level of heat-trapping gases in the atmosphere," said the Friz. "Heat-trapping gases are also called greenhouse gases."
She had that funny gleam in her eye.
We could tell something "interesting" was about to happen.

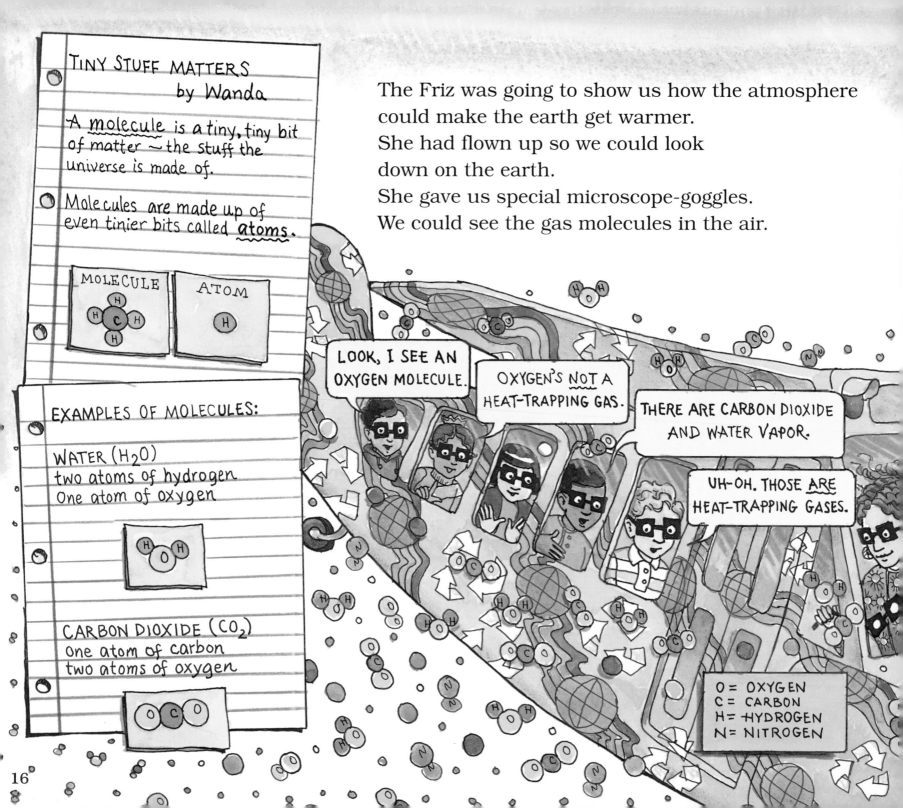

The Friz was going to show us how the atmosphere could make the earth get warmer.
She had flown up so we could look down on the earth.
She gave us special microscope-goggles.
We could see the gas molecules in the air.

16

21

Our teacher shooed us back on the bus-plane. Like it or not, we were on our way to see some alternative energy.

TONS OF CO_2
by Keesha
Q: How much CO_2 goes into the atmosphere for each person in the U.S.?
A: Too much!
About 44,000 pounds a year. That's the same as eight hefty hippos per person every year!

REDUCING CO_2 ~
WHAT'S OUR GOAL?
By the year 2050, Americans should have reduced their hippos a lot. Instead of eight hippos, an American should emit less than one hippo per year.

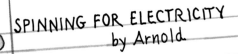

SPINNING FOR ELECTRICITY
by Arnold

Generators have turbines, or blades, that spin. The spinning movement reacts with magnets to make electric current.

We set out to see generators—
machines that make electricity.
Most generators burn fossil fuel to spin
their turbines and make electricity.
Alternative generators make it without fossil fuels.

TURBINE   GENERATOR

BLADES SPINNING   TURN SHAFT   SPIN MAGNETS

ELECTRIC CURRENT

LOOK AT ALL THE THINGS THAT ARE MAKING ELECTRICITY.

AND NO GREENHOUSE GASES.

HYDROELECTRIC PLANT
Movement of water over a dam spins turbines in a generator.

DAM
GENERATOR
TURBINE

GEOTHERMAL PLANT
Heat from inside the earth makes steam to move turbines.

STEAM

NUCLEAR-ELECTRIC PLANT
Heat made in nuclear reactors does the same thing.

STEAM
NUCLEAR REACTOR
COOLING TOWER

As we flew over a desert, we heard a loud crunch.
Out the window, we saw the bus-plane's wings fall off!
"Ms. Frizzle!" we yelled, but she didn't seem to notice.
She was too busy telling us about more
alternative energy.
This time she pointed to a huge
solar generator below.

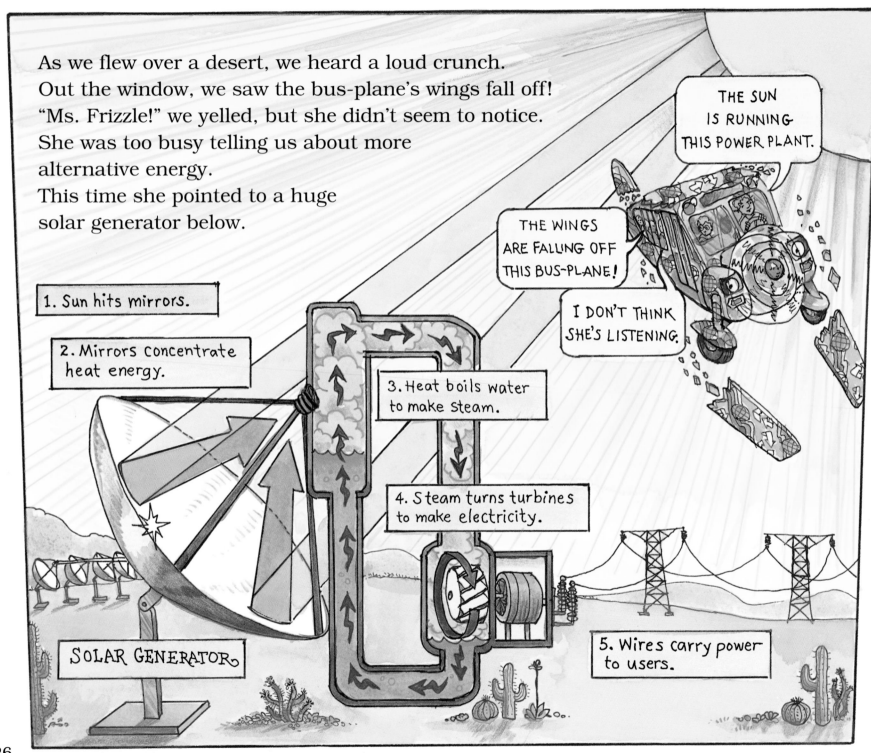

The bus made a crash landing.
Oops, we mean a *splash* landing.
We were floating in a solar-heated swimming pool.
Ms. Frizzle kept talking, telling us about solar cells.
They make energy directly from the sun—
with no moving parts.

The bus stopped being a pool toy, so we rode into town.
Everywhere, people were saving energy. Instead of driving private cars, many were using trains, buses, taxis, and bikes, as well as more fuel-efficient vehicles.

Ms. Frizzle pulled a bright green lever. At once the bus morphed into a hybrid vehicle that ran on gasoline and a rechargeable battery.

"Can we please go back to school, Ms. Frizzle?" we begged. "We've been on this bus too long!" For once our teacher listened.

MORE WORDS FROM DOROTHY ANN

A HYBRID VEHICLE uses more than one source of energy.

A FUEL-EFFICIENT vehicle uses less fuel to go more miles.

KIDS CAN...
Take the school bus instead of being driven by a parent.

EVEN AN INEFFICIENT SCHOOL BUS EMITS LESS CO_2 THAN 20 CARS DRIVING KIDS TO SCHOOL.

KIDS CAN... Ask adults to stop letting vehicles idle.

PLEASE TURN OFF YOUR ENGINE WHILE WAITING.

WALKING PATH

HIKE AND BIKE!

GO GREEN!

BIKE PATH

30

We had to start saving energy right away.
"Conserve, conserve, conserve!" shouted the Friz.
"Recycle, recycle, recycle!"

MORE WORDS FROM D.A.

Conserve means to avoid waste.

Recycle means to treat waste materials so they can be used again.

RECYCLING SAVES ENERGY
by Tim

Making new cans from recycled cans uses 30% less energy than making them from new aluminum.

KIDS CAN...
Recycle cans and bottles!

A LITTLE CAN DO A LOT
If your town recycled 2,000 pounds of aluminum cans, it would save enough energy to heat the typical home for 10 years.

We started making changes at our school.
There was plenty of room for improvement.
Then we called the mayor of our town.
Then we wrote to the president.

We told everyone, "Let's cut down on greenhouse gases now!"

:: Don't leave the fridge open too long.
:: Buy Energy Star appliances.

IT'S NOT COOL TO LEAVE THE FRIDGE OPEN!

ENERGY STAR

:: Buy things with less packaging.
:: Buying MORE local produce...

...SAVES ON PACKAGING AND TRANSPORTATION.

:: Use cloth shopping bags.
:: Buy LESS bottled water.

:: Air-dry your laundry.

A LITTLE CAN DO A LOT
If every household in the U.S. switched three lights to compact fluorescent lamps (CFLS), it would reduce as much CO_2 as taking 3.5 million cars off the road.

That's because old incandescent bulbs waste a lot of energy making heat. CFLS use most of their energy making light.

THE LESS ENERGY YOU USE, THE LESS CO_2 GOES INTO THE AIR.

Finally, we had time to put on our play.
It was about everything we had seen on our trip.
We showed what global warming was doing to our planet.
And we told about how people can help.

Can you believe it?
A TV station found out about us,
and we got to be on television!

37

QUESTIONS FOR MS. FRIZZLE'S CLASS
... an online chat

Q. Can a class really go up in the sky and ride sunbeams into the earth?
from IvannaNO@once.now

A. According to our research, only Ms. Frizzle's class can do that.
from Dorothy.Ann@a.loss.to.explain.net

Q. Why are you so worried about global warming? There were warm times in Earth's past, weren't there?
from Onceupon@time.now

A. In past times, Earth's climate has been cool, cold, warm, and hot. But these changes have happened over millions of years. Animals and plants had time to adjust. The warming we see now has happened in only a few hundred years. We can't adapt that fast.
from Ralphie@a.gallop.net

Q. Can a single person really change things?
from Juan@atime4change.net

A. One individual can't make a big difference.
But millions of individuals can!
from Phoebe@longlast/together.net

Q. Don't we need bigger help?
from a.giant@least?.net

A. You're right. We need all the governments of the
world to cooperate in solving the climate crisis.
from Ms.Frizzle@the.crossroads

Q. Why does Ms. Frizzle always go on such
weird class trips?
from kids@risk?safety.net

A. That's what I would like to know.
from Arnold@home.sweet.home